WHISPERS

IN THE WIND

My splendid son-in-law +
~ Son of Hyram and Joan Eisenstein ~

DOUGLAS R. EISENSTEIN

Based upon
THE WORLD WAR I MEMOIRS OF
SERGEANT JACK L. HORN
And
CAPTAIN W. KERR RAINSFORD
307TH INFANTRY
77TH DIVISION
NATIONAL ARMY
1917

With an introduction by Sergeant Horn's Son
Paul Horn

The Forum

AT TUCSON

Library of Congress Number: 00-192860
ISBN #:   Hardcover   0-7388-4945-6
                 Softcover   0-7388-4946-4

This book was printed in the United States of America.

To order additional copies of this book, contact:
Xlibris Corporation
1-888-7-XLIBRIS
www.Xlibris.com
Orders@Xlibris.com

CONTENTS

To all the millions who were never born

From Mr. Horn's Son

My father, Jack Leonard Horn, was born in New York City on November 5, 1895 and died on November 2, 1981. His parents emigrated from Hungary in 1893 and set themselves up in the restaurant business. His mother died when he was two years old. His two older brothers and one sister went to an orphanage and he grew up in foster homes. His father visited him on weekends. Dad went to work while attending night school. He received his high school diploma this way and finished two years of college before he was drafted into the army during World War I on July 20, 1917. As an infantry sergeant on the front lines, he had to lead soldiers out of the trenches over the top, through No Man's Land, and into hand-to-hand combat with the Germans. He was discharged on May 9, 1919. Shortly afterwards he discovered that he had tuberculosis as a result of inhalation of mustard gas. He spent two years in a sanitarium in upstate New York. During this time he recovered completely and met my mother. They were married in 1929.

Dad was an honest and charming man. He liked people and people liked him. As a result he was in sales most of his life and was successful and happy in that profession. He was quiet and low-key and had a great sense of humor. He was a very loving man. He had tremendous inner strength, which allowed him to be soft. Things touched him deeply because of his sensitivity. Tears came to his eyes easily, not from sadness, but from the beauty and poignancy he saw in life. He was a straight-ahead guy who did not like discord, violence, or anything upsetting. I don't remember any yelling or heavy arguments between my mother and father.

He did not intellectualize much or indulge in philosophical discussions. Having survived the horrendous experiences he had in the war, which are detailed in his diary, and seeing death all around him at such an early age, automatically instilled in him the deeper meaning of life. He lived this understanding and appreciation daily. All those who knew him and were touched by his beautiful soul had their souls enriched in return.

The story in this book offers much more than a daily account of an infantryman on the front lines during WWI. It is a chronicle of the times. It gives an insight into how Americans felt about their country and their willingness to make the ultimate sacrifice to preserve our freedoms. There was a great national PRIDE.

In a way the situation was black and white. There was an obvious enemy that must be destroyed. The good guys were readily distinguished from the bad guys. They even had uniforms by which one could easily recognize the enemy. When the fighting was hand to hand, you looked into the eyes of the person you were killing. There was true victory and defeat.

Throughout the rest of the twentieth century this distinction between good guys and bad guys has become more and more blurred. Innocent civilians have increasingly become the targets and bombs and missiles are dropped without ever seeing the people dying. At the end of it all there is no true victory and many are left wondering what it was all about.

My father loved this country until the day he died and was forever proud that he had the opportunity to serve in the cause of freedom. Above his bed were two American flags crossed. Beneath that was a picture of his company (used as this book's cover). He was seated in the front row center. Most of the men in that picture never made it home. I think that must have served as a daily reminder of his good fortune and never to take the gift of life for granted.

Paul Horn
Tucson, Arizona
2000

ACKNOWLEDGEMENTS

Special thanks to Lisa L. Wong for painstakingly transcribing the original journals to print. This was no easy task since the diary (in remarkable condition for the most part) is over 80 years old. There were no ball point pens in those days. The ink in many places is smeared or faded almost beyond recognition due to the rain and generally wet conditions on the front lines. That Mr. Horn even kept a daily journal through all this is remarkable. Thanks to my friend Paul Horn for his enthusiastic help with this project. Also, thank-you to my wife, Jennifer, my best friend.

SEVENTY-SEVENTH DIVISION

Named the "Metropolitan Division" owing to its origins. The insignia was a gold Statue of Liberty on a truncated triangle of flag blues. It was organized on August 30, 1917 at Camp Upton. The majority of the enlisted men were from New York City and Long Island, New York. On October 10, 1917, many of the men were transferred to Camp Upton and Camp Greenwood, the vacancies caused thereby being filled by men from Camp Devens, Mass., and from Northern New York State. The division began leaving Camp Upton on March 28, 1918, and sailed from Boston, Portland (Maine), via Halifax and New York City. With the exception of the artillery, all units proceeded through Liverpool, across England and landed at Calais, France. The artillery sailed from New York in April and went directly to Brest, France.

The division moved immediately to a training area in back of the British front near St. Omer and while being trained by the 39th British Division, was held in reserve to meet the anticipated German attack against the channel ports, which never materialized. The artillery brigade on arrival moved to an American training area at Souges. On June 16, 1918, the division moved by train to the Baccarat sector. On July 12, 1918, the artillery brigade relieved the French artillery in the Baccarat sector. During the time spent in this sector the division held a broad frontage.

On August 4, 1918 the division moved to the Vesle sector in the neighborhood of Fismes, on August 11, entering the line. With French troops on both flanks and forming a part of the 6th French Army, the division commenced the attack of the German positions north of the River Vesle on August 18, crossing the Vesle on September 5, and advanced its left flank to the River Aisne. The division was relieved September 15, moving for two days rest to the region of Arcyle-Poin Sart. The Division began moving September 17 by bus and marching to St. Menehould. On September 21, elements of the division moved into position in the Argonne trenches. By September 25 the whole division was in position and on September 26 attacked on the left of the 1st American Army in the Argonne forest. On October 15 and 16, the Division was relieved and concentrated in the vicinity east of Cornay (1st Corps Reserve) where it was held in readiness for immediate use if required. During this time the division troops were employed in reorganizing the line of defense. On October 25, the Division relieved a line division and continued in the attack until November 12, advancing from St. Juvin to the Meuse. The Division was relieved November 12 and moved to the vicinity of Les Vignettes on November 21, and thence proceeded on November 30 to the 9th training area and established division headquarters at Chateau Villain.

The Division captured from the enemy the following: 13 officers, 737 men, 44 pieces of artillery, 323 machine guns and numerous supplies. The 77th Division made a total advance against resistance of 71.5 kilometers. Battle deaths,

1,990; wounded, 9,966; prisoners of war, 404. Distinguished Service Crosses awarded 146.

Commanding General: Major General J. Franklin Bell, August 18, 1917 to May 18, 1918; Major General George B. Duncan, May 18 to August 24, 1918; Brigadier General Evan M. Johnson, August 24 to August 31, 1918; Major General Robert Alexander, August 31 to November 11, 1918.

The units comprising the 77th Division were as follows:

153rd, 154th Infantry Brigades
305th, 306th, 307th, 308th Infantry Regiments
305th Machine Gun Battalion
152nd Artillery Brigade
304th, 305th, 306th Artillery Regiments
302nd Trench Mortar Battery
304th Division Machine Gun Battalion
302nd Engineers Regiment and Train
302nd Field. Signal Battalion
302nd Train Headquarters
302nd Supply Train
302nd Ammunition Train
302nd Sanitary Train
305th, 306th, 307th, 308th Ambulance Companies and Field Hospitals

The well-known "Lost Battalion" was a part of the 308th Infantry of this division.

National Army
2nd Army Corps
77th Division (Upton)—Major General George B. Duncan, commanding;

Major W. N. Haskell, Adjutant-General
- 153rd Brigade Infantry—Brigadier General Edward Wittenmayer
  - 305th Infantry Regiment
  - 306th Infantry Regiment
  - 305th Machine Gun Battalion
- 154th Brigade Infantry—Brigadier General Evan M. Johnson
  - 307th Infantry Regiment
  - 308th Infantry Regiment
  - 306th Machine Gun Battalion
- 152nd Brigade, Field Artillery—Brigadier General Thomas H. Reeves
  - 304th Field Artillery Regiment
  - 305th Field Artillery Regiment
  - 306th Field Artillery Regiment
  - 302nd Trench Mortar Battery
- Engineer Troops–302nd Regiment
- Signal Troops–302nd Battalion
- Division Units—77th Division Headquarters Troop; 304th Machine Gun Battalion.

Introduction

The First World War was pointless. There was no clear-cut villain threatening to dominate the world. No unprovoked aggressive ideologies being imposed on unwilling others. No world supply of needed resources being threatened. No religious or ethnic group was targeted for complete annihilation. It was a war fought mostly by boys in their teens and men in their early twenties, far away from home for an obscure cause. Yet despite all of these considerations, ten million lives were lost in this war. The British lost 1 million. The French lost 2 million or 2 out of every 9 soldiers who went. Of these, 630,000 were newlyweds who had not yet had the chance to produce children. Serbia suffered the loss of 45,000 lives out of a total population of 5 million. Rumania suffered the most proportionately; of the 750,000 men that went to war 350,000, or 45%, were killed. Germany lost 2,057,000 lives. Russia sacrificed 1.7 million, Italy 460,000, Austria 1.5 million. The United States suffered much less than the other combatants with 116,708 deaths. This was because of its late arrival, 3 years after the war had begun.

The losses of Britain include Australia and New Zealand known as ANZAC (Australian New Zealand Army Corp) who fought valiantly and tragically at Gallipoli.

These numbers cannot help but to give pause for melancholy reflection. The resultant loss of the progeny these men would have produced has cast a long shadow over the 20th century. We will never know how many scientists, artists, musicians, writers, entertainers and influential leaders would have existed had this war not taken its toll. While the same can be said for all wars to a greater or lesser extent, this particular war is most poignant due to the senselessness of the slaughter.

World War I was a tragedy whose scope defies comprehension. It marked the beginning of modern warfare, but with a profound difference. It was modern in that the means to inflict mass death and destruction were available for the first time, but the means to control and focus this devastation were primitive. The political and military leaders of the time were like children who discover too late the dangers of playing with matches. Once the fire has begun, it cannot be easily stopped, cannot be directed, and therefore its effects cannot be limited or controlled. The leaders of the time had at their disposal huge armies with vast destructive arsenals but no way to effectively direct them. For this kind of power to be effective one must be able to direct and focus it; turn it on at precisely the right moment, redirect it when off-target so as to avoid your own troops striking only the enemy and terminate it immediately when success or failure is imminent. Without this instantaneous feedback the war machine was a vicious, thrashing, indiscriminate beast without a brain. Added to this random killing was the introduction of poison gas which, when released, would hopefully drift upon the wayward breezes in the direction of the enemy. If the wind shifted, as it often did, the attackers would quickly become the victims.

The obvious method of instantaneous communication is

with wireless devices, but this technology was in its infancy and went virtually unused in this war. The potential benefits of its use were recognized, but the wireless devices of the time were cumbersome and heavy and therefore not suitable for mobile field use. They also required high amounts of electricity, which was available only in metropolitan areas. Battery technology was essentially nonexistent. As command posts were at a safe distance miles away and headquarters were farther yet, the information needed to make decisions was slow in coming. Once the information was received the resulting directives often took hours to make their way back to the front lines. Commanding officers did have telephones at their disposal, but these used delicate wires, which were immediately severed at the onset of battle. Therefore information had to be conveyed in both directions by carrier pigeons, dogs and human runners. These methods proved to be tragically ineffectual. Pleas for reinforcements, or requests to redirect artillery fire away from your own forces, if they are received at all, require instantaneous attention. But it would usually take hours. The loss of life from this deficiency alone is incalculable.

The origins of the First World War can be traced to this inability to communicate. At all times during the weeks leading up to the war the decision to escalate hostilities or defuse the entire process was in the hands of no more than five leaders; Czar Nicolas II of Russia, Emperor Franz Josef of Austria, Kaiser Wilhelm II of Germany, President Raymond Poincaré of France and King George V of Great Britain. Had these men, or their ministers and ambassadors, been able to talk to each other directly in "real time" the train of events which ultimately led to war might have been broken. Instead they were forced to rely on couriers carrying messages over vast distances or telegrams wired over undependable lines. Telegrams, once received, had to then be carried to the intended recipient. Often a conciliatory message arrived too late to alter decisions that had already been set in motion.

This deficiency of rapid communication allowed events to progress inexorably in domino fashion. In the short period of only a few weeks Europe was at war. This progression of events was, ironically, made easier by a series of treaties and agreements which were originally intended to prevent such a conflagration.

Technically, the war lasted from August 4, 1914 to November 11, 1918, but it really began in Sarajevo, Bosnia at 11 o'clock in the morning on June 28, 1914. On that date, Gravilo Princip, a Serbian nationalist, shot and killed Archduke Franz Ferdinand, nephew of Emperor Franz Josef of Austria and heir to the throne. The Archduke's wife, Sophie, was also killed at point blank range. This assassination triggered a progression of events, which, over the ensuing six weeks resulted in war. Austria-Hungary wanted revenge on Serbia but lacked the confidence to launch a strike on her own. Had she done so, the conflict most likely would have remained localized between Serbia and Austria-Hungary. Instead, Austria-Hungary sought and received Germany's assurance to support the attack on Serbia. Russia had a strong fondness for Serbia and pledged to defend it by attacking Austria. Germany then mobilized its forces for an attack on Russia to defend Austria.

Mobilization of Germany against Russia triggered the Franco-Russian treaty of 1892 wherein France and Russia agreed upon mutual defense against any aggressors. France therefore began to mobilize against Germany. This resulted in Germany declaring war on France. This in turn vitalized an agreement between Great Britain and France wherein they would come to each other's aid if the national interests of either country were threatened. Great Britain therefore mobilized against Germany.

Germany, Austria-Hungary and Italy had what was called the Triple Alliance Treaty. This treaty pledged that these three nations would come to each other's aid should any one of them be threatened by no less than two other countries. France, Russia and Great Britain now threatened Germany. Italy delayed but eventually entered the war.

This powder keg exploded in the first week of August 1914 resulting in the Great War.

World War I was fought primarily on two fronts; the Western Front and the Eastern Front. The Eastern Front was 500 miles long extending from the border of Germany and Russia at the Baltic sea, south to the border of Romania. It was the Western front where the A.E.F. (American Expeditionary Force) fought alongside the French and British forces. The Western front extended for 475 miles from the coast of the North Sea beginning in Nieuport, Belgium, across France through the very dense Argonne Forest to the border of Switzerland near the village of Bonfol.

America remained neutral for the first three years of the war. There is a common misconception that U.S. involvement resulted from the sinking of the *Lusitania*. That tragic event occurred in May of 1915, a full two years before America's arrival, and because of it Germany promised to only target naval ships. The U.S. was actually drawn into the war by two other events. The first was an ill-advised attempt in February of 1917 by Germany to establish an alliance with Mexico. In exchange for this, Germany promised to return Texas, Arizona and New Mexico upon America's defeat. The second event was the announcement by Germany that they were going to resume attacks on all ships in international waters. This was to include civilian and merchant ships. The sinking of the Cunard liner *Laconia* on February 26, 1917 by a German U-boat was the final provocation.

The first American forces arrived on June 25, 1917. The 77th Division, of which the 307th Regiment was a part, arrived at Calais, France on April 20, 1918. As was the case with the other newly arrived A.E.F. divisions, the 77th Division used quiet areas along the Western Front far behind the line for training and drilling. After several months of this intensive training, the next phase was to station the troops at relatively inactive sectors along the front. During this phase they would serve alongside the French and British troops. This would allow some time to develop a mutual *esprit de corps* with the "foreign troops" and a familiarization with the different language, culture, and military discipline. The last phase of their training was to occupy sections of their own along the Front. There were times during heavy fighting when troops would be sent directly from behind the line training to active combat. After a division had been involved in active fighting they were, depending on their casualty toll, rotated back to the more quiet training zones for reorganization, additional training and rest.

While America joined the war late in its course, it was decisive in its outcome. At the beginning of 1918 the French and British armies were exhausted and badly weakened after almost three years of fighting. The French had suffered costly defeats and the army was mired in mutiny. To make matters worse, Russia, under Lenin, had withdrawn from the war handing Germany victory on the Eastern Front. This freed up over 1 million additional German soldiers to be transferred to the Western Front. The earliest U.S. forces immediately took over the quiet sectors of the line freeing French and British troops to deploy where they were more urgently needed. As wave after wave of U.S. troops arrived, they began to occupy the sectors where active fighting was occurring greatly boosting French and British morale. The Germans began to weaken suffering setback after setback.

The 307th Regiment was involved in two major and decisive battles in 1918; the Meuse-Argonne Offensive, fought in the nightmarish, dense tangle of the Argonne Forest and the Oise-Aisne Offensive.

* * *

This book is a true story in the purest sense of the phrase. It is an eyewitness account of one U.S. soldier's involvement in World War I. Jack Horn was a foot soldier who meticulously maintained a daily diary from his days in boot camp beginning September 22, 1917 through his return home to New York May 9, 1919. The diary was kept in three small volumes, which not only survived the harrowing experience of war and weather but also the eighty plus years since they were penned. The original grammar, spelling and punctuation have been preserved as written.

The diary came to my attention one evening during after-dinner conversation with my dear friend Paul Horn, Jack Horn's son. We were discussing the memorabilia he has accumulated over his remarkable career as a world famous jazz musician. I asked about the photograph of his father which appears in one of Paul's many recording albums. His father's World War I uniform intrigued me. Paul mentioned that he found the photo among some of his father's possessions, which included the three diaries. He had never really been able to sit down and read them due to the poor condition of the ink. Water and in some cases blood had smeared the words which were already cramped and often unsteady.

Being interested in all things historical, especially old photographs and personal accounts of historic events, I was immediately enthused. I told Paul that these diaries must be transcribed so that the words could be preserved and more easily shared.

We showed the diaries to expert transcriptionist Lisa Wong who, after careful study of the delicate little volumes, gallantly offered to transcribe them. Almost one year later her gallantry had been replaced by dogged determination seeing the job through to its completion.

Having the writings in a more useable form, I was able to set about footnoting every reference Mr. Horn made to people, places and things that I felt would not be known to the majority of readers. Research then followed to uncover the details of all that had been mentioned in the diary. My original plan had been to publish the work after this stage was complete with some accompanying photos and historical perspective. But an amazing bit of luck came my way. After most of the research had been completed, I was demonstrating to a friend the power of the various search engines available on the internet. So at random I typed in "307th Regiment" to show him the wealth of references with which we would quickly be deluged. As predicted, dozens of references came up relating to regiments, which had had this number from the time of Napoleon's campaigns to the Vietnam War. Among this long list one particular reference caught my eye: *From Upton to the Meuse with the Three Hundred and Seventh* by W. Kerr Rainsford. Having practically eaten, slept and drank this diary for over a year, the words "Upton", which served as Mr. Horn's boot camp, and "Meuse", the French river where the final German engagements occurred, were, by now, shockingly familiar to me. Clicking on this particular reference took me to the New York State Library, Education Department. The above link referred to a book, which had been written in 1920 by a captain of the 307th Regiment of the 77th Division of the National Army. The same regiment Mr. Horn was in. No further information was available online. I called the New York State Library and ended up speaking to Dawn Tybur who turned out to be one of those wonderful librarians most of us fondly remember from our youth; the kind who will pursue your request for a bit of information with the determination of a terrier.

After some days of searching she informed me that only a few copies of this book existed and that the New York State Library did not have a copy. However . . . she had found a copy in the Sam Houston State University Library in Huntsville, Texas. She then sent me detailed information on how to obtain the book through an inter-library loan program.

Within two weeks I was holding the book in my hands and it was better than I had hoped. The book was also a diary of sorts that Captain Rainsford had kept during the exact same period of time that Corporal Horn had been keeping his. Beginning on Long Island at the boot camp (Camp Upton) to the return to New York City twenty months later.

Suddenly all of the places and events that I had only known from Mr. Horn's perspective, were seen in an entirely new light. Captain Rainsford graduated from Harvard in 1904 and his writing reflected the quality of his education, it was precise and detailed. He, of course, had some advantages that Mr. Horn did not. His day to day conditions were probably considerably more comfortable. Mr. Horn often had to write his daily accounts outside in the rain up to his knees in mud while being bombarded by artillery and sniped at by rifle fire. This is not to say that the officers were not exposed to just as much danger. Indeed post-war statistics indicate that the heaviest casualty rates were among the regular officers at 25 percent compared to 14 percent for the enlisted men. In fact, Captain Rainsford was wounded in August, 1918, hospitalized, returned to duty in September and again severely wounded in October, 1918, again hospitalized, and returned to duty in December.

Having the two works side by side made the disparity between the perspective of the foot soldier compared to the officer profoundly clear. From the soldier's point of view, as is reflected in Mr. Horn's diary, the days and weeks were composed of hikes and marches to unknown destinations for unknown reasons. Mr. Rainsford, as a senior officer, knew exactly what was planned each day and how it fit into the larger picture of positioning the troops according to the changing enemy positions. The foot soldier might happily start the day only knowing that they were going to march fifteen miles before dusk, while the officers were aware that by dusk they could be taking heavy casualties at the hands of the enemy. There was, of course, logic to this. Soldiers are commonly captured and the less they know the better for themselves as well as the remaining men. Also there was little to be gained by telling a relaxed soldier in the morning that he would be facing death by that evening. Thus, the Captain's memoirs fill in the details that were unavailable to Mr. Horn.

The writings that follow are the story of one regiment's experiences from the languid days of boot camp to the more intensive behind the lines training in France to the final costly battles leading to victory and the return home. There were days, weeks and months of monotonous, boring tedium mixed with days, weeks and months of unrelenting terror and death.

A word about the structure of the main body of this book. There are three voices. The full margin regular typeset is the writings of Mr. Horn. The reduced margin bold typeset is the writings of Mr. Rainsford. The italicized typeset is my writing.

World War I was a cold, raging wind that blew across Europe and the world. Here are the whispers of two voices in that wind.

The First World War was a tragic and unnecessary conflict.

John Keegan,
The First World War

"I sank down upon my knees and thanked Heaven out of the fullness of my heart for the favor of having been permitted to live in such times."

Adolph Hitler,
(Describing his reaction upon hearing Germany's proclamation of war, Munich, 1914)

Volume I

September 22, 1917 to November 6, 1917

Registered June 5, 1917
Drafted July 20, 1917 Friday

To Jack L. Horn[1]
From Leo J. Horn
Sept. 3, 1917

Sept. 22, 1917
Prvt. Jack L. Horn
958 Prospect Ave
Bronx, N.Y.C.

Company Dee{*sic*}
Regiment 307th Infantry

No. of my gun—5494

Before commencing this diary, I wish to make note of the events, which lead up to the life I will live from now on, as a soldier.

President Wilson issued a proclamation on April 8, 1917 that war exists between this country and Germany. (*see Appendix I*). Later congress voted that June 5th is set a side{*sic*} as registration day for the selection draft of all men between the ages of 21 and 31.

July 20th was draft day and my red ink number 982 was the 761st number pulled from a glass recepticle{*sic*} at Washington. This placed me 269 on the list in my district.

After being called for physical examination and found physically fit my standing was 81 on the accepted list in my local exemption board # 11. I asked my local board to send me to Yapchank{*sic*}[2], our future mining camp, as soon as possible and shortly after received both my green and red cards in rapid succession.

Sept 22, 1917

I reported to my local board this day at 7 A.M. and left for the Penn station with 41 other drafted men of my district. Left at 11 A.M. and arrived at Camp Upton[3] about 1:30 P.M.

The 307th Infantry, 154th Brigade, 77th Division, National Army, came into confused being at camp Upton, Long Island, with the first increment of the draft from New York, in September, 1917. Its enlisted personnel was very largely from the East Side of the city, and contained every nationality that America has welcomed to her shores, but almost none who, on any pretext, had handled a rifle; its camp site was a recently cleared area of dust or mud, according to the weather.

Arriving at our barrock{*sic*} R24 we registered and were given two blankets, a mess kit and a mattress cover. About 2:00 P.M. we tasted our first army meal and were well pleased with same. I filled my mattress with hay in the afternoon and took a shower bath towards evening.

Sept 23, 1917

Awoke at 5:30 A.M. Cold and sleepy but after a cold wash felt as strong and healthy as a Sampson. After breakfast, we were taken to the hospital for another examination and past{*sic*} same with ease. We were then vaccinated and inocculated{*sic*} with typhoid germs. After being mustered in we were permitted to rest for the balance of the day. Felt a little weak from the inocculation{*sic*} and spent most of the day in my bunk.

Sept 24th

Awoke at 5:30 A.M. Washed and dressed and fell in line for roll call at 5:45.

Breakfast at 6:00. After breakfast we were told to pack all our belongings in a blanket and be ready to move. I was transfered{*sic*} to Company D. 307th Infantry. Barrock{*sic*} P.76.

> The company officers had expected to encounter difficulties in their appointed tasks, and they did so, but not as they had anticipated. The draft arrived in groups of thirty to sixty or more, usually following behind a box-standard bearing the number of the Local Board, and in charge of a temporary leader, who submitted a list of their names and an armful of their appropriate papers. While the receiving officer, on the steps of his

barracks, was ascertaining the innumerable dis-
crepancies between the two, the draft stood about
eyeing him with expectant curiosity, with friendly
amusement, with critical displeasure, or with apa-
thy, according to their nationality or mood—with
any and every emotion save military respect. Then
came the calling of the role and further discrep-
ancies. Certain men would answer with alacrity,
to each of three names called, or stand silent while
their own was called as many times. As a typical
instance, a man in Company M had answered
"Here" at every formation for nearly a week before he was discovered to have been left at home
on account of illness, and never to have reported
at the camp. Another ghost was laid to rest by
the following dialogue:
"Mora, T."
"Here."
"Mora, R."
"Here." (from the same individual)
"Does your first name begin with a T or an R? "
"Yes, sir."
"Is your first name Rocco?"
"Yes, sir."
"What is your first name?"
"Tony."

After getting settled in my new quarters, I went down for
mess and when I finished my first meal in my new barrocks{*sic*}
I was so well pleased I hoped I would remain here.

Sept 25, 1917

To-day being a Jewish Holiday[4], All Jews were given
permission to go home to attend the services. I left after mess

and caught the 2 o'clock train for N.Y. Arrived home about 4:30 P.M. and was glad to see the folks again. Spent the rest of the day with my friends and returned the next day to Camp Upton boarding the midnight train.

Sept 27, 1917

Received part of our uniforms to-day

> Then came the fitting of uniforms. One set of all possible sizes was available for trying on to each battalion, though not often to any of its companies; the consolidated requisitions were made out and submitted, and were filled, of necessity, piecemeal in the course of days or weeks; by which time the casuals[5] had largely been sent to other organizations, and others, coming from elsewhere, had taken their place. These brought with them memoranda of their required sizes, or had lost them, as the case might be. It was the usual experience that the sizes noted were not the sizes required, that the sizes received were very possibly not the sizes requisitioned, and that the articles had probably been marked with the wrong sizes in the first instance.

and also went on a long hike and received our first drill lesson. Was put to work stuffing mattresses in the afternoon for the new recruits that are expected to-day. We were not permitted to leave the barrocks{sic} this evening because we did not have our complete uniforms and were expecting same to-night.

Sept 28, 1917

Received the balance of our uniforms this morning and put them on immediately. Spent the balance of the morning fussing up and complimenting each other on our fine appearance.

In the afternoon we lined up for drill and looked like a fine lot of soldiers. I was appointed acting Corporal

> But by this time the good material was coming to the fore. Corporals and sergeants had been found who could take hold of their men, drill them, and enforce regulations; and there never was any apparent unwillingness on the part of the enlisted men to serve, nor conscious wish to deny authority.

by the Captain because of my previous military experience at Governors Island[6]{*sic*}.

Sept 30

After spending a restful Sunday we were prepared for a strenuous week. Directly after mess in the morning we hiked out to the parade grounds

> The training of the companies was made difficult by the lateness of the season and the lack of any adequate drill-ground or gymnasium. As the mud became more universal and deeper the few macadamized roads became attractive for the drilling of squads and for close order march; but the consequent interference with traffic led to this being strictly prohibited. Troops were forbidden to move at any time in greater frontage than columns of twos upon the hard roads.

and had our "setting up" exercises and drills. In the afternoon we had our first lessons in trench digging and were
complemented{*sic*} upon our good work.

Oct 2, 1917
Things are running along smoothly and upon schedule.
We have our exercises and drills in the morning and the afternoon is generally devoted to lessons in the semephora {*sic*}
drill[7], which is a two arm signal drill. And occassionaly{*sic*} we
are sent out into the woods to clear away the shrubly{*sic*} and
chop down trees besides these drills.

October 4, 1917
The morning passed away in the usual manner, but in the
afternoon, instead of having semephora drill, we were marched
to Regemental{*sic*} Headquarters and there we received our
second typhoid inocculation{*sic*}. It was my turn to do guard
duty for the night, and being corporal of the guard I had a six
hour shift (from 12:30 A.M. to 6:30

A.M.) I was in continual fever from the inocculation{*sic*}
throughout the night and welcomed the revillie{*sic*} call.

Oct 7, 1917
Have fully recovered from my inocculation{*sic*} and re-
ceived permission to go home to spend the week end in the
City. Left camp on the 1:30 train which was so crowded that
I was compelled to stand all the way to N.Y.

The nearness of New York, however, while a convenience to the individual, was a decidedly ad-
verse factor to discipline and control; and the
men, except those from up-state, never quite cut

> loose from the city nor gave themselves unre-
> servedly to the military life. The difficulty of
> A.W.O.L. (absence without leave) was pro-
> nounced throughout the entire period at Camp
> Upton, and that of drunkenness, while not acute,
> was always to be reckoned with.

And as luck would have it something happened to the engine and the train took four and a half hours to reach its destination instead of two. Spent a quiet Sunday at home.

Oct 10, 1917

Received our usual drill and exercises in the morning. Wednesday is generally our afternoon off, but as we expected to receive our first pay to-day, we were told to remain in the barrocks{sic}. While we were waiting, we ran out occassionally{sic} to look at a near by score board to learn the score of the Giants—White Sox game. The Giants won 2 to 0. We did not receive our pay until 5:30 P.M.

Oct 16, 1917

Directly alter mess this morning we marched out to our future parade grounds and worked there all morning clearing the place of brush wood and logs. About 2 o'clock in the afternoon I was inocculated{sic} for the third time and as I lied in my bunk, I was called to the orderly room to report to our Captain. He scolded me for the poor condition of the barrocks{sic} last Saturday when I was in charge of Quarters and also because I left camp without permission Saturday night. He sentenced me to two weeks confinement to my barrocks{sic}. I accepted my punishment as a soldier should.

Oct 24, 1917

To-day was declared a holiday and it was called "Liberty Bond Day"[8]. It is the last day that we can subscribe for the second liberty Loan. It proved to be a miserable day. It is raining heavily and a strong wind is blowing. This morning I received a long distance call from my brother Leo in the city and was pleased to speak to him. This afternoon we were shifted so that all our squad is bunked to-gether{*sic*}. I am now in the twelfth squad.

Oct 25, 1917

After drill this morning we were assembled in the mess hall to sign a permission to deduct from our salary five dollars for every Liberty Bond for which we subscribed. This evening I sneaked out of the barrocks{*sic*} for a short stroll. I finally decided to look up my friend Henry Goldenberg. When I met him, I was astonished to learn that he was being transferred to Camp Gordon, Georgia[9].

Camp Gordon, strangely in need of men, offered a certain safety-valve, and the man whose face seemed irreconcilable with a steel helmet, whose name on the roll-call consisted only of consonants, or who had cast his rice pudding in the mess sergeant's face often completed his training there—on the pretext that all is fair in war.

I spent the balance of the night bidding him Good-bye and reported to my barrocks{*sic*} 6:00 A.M.

Oct 28

To-day is Saturday and inspection day. We are all dressed spick and span. One would never suspect from our appearance that we were hard working, stump digging soldiers. At 9:30 this morning we had our first parade of the battalion and of course felt proud and cocky and made a good showing. This afternoon is my day off and I watch our company suffer defeat at the hands of Co. B. at a game of baseball.

Oct 31

We were scheduled for a twelve mile hike this morning. When we arose the sky was dark and the air very chilly. Immediately after mess we lined up and marched to the open field for our morning exercises with the hopes that it would warm us up. About 8:30 A.M. our battalion started off on the hike. Everything ran smoothly until we were about two or three miles from camp. Then we were attacked by a heavy storm and marched back. Soaked through to the skin and suffering our first defeat by the rain.

Nov 6

I was awakened a half hour earlier this morning with the rest of the company and told to dress hurriedly and report in the mess hall. I noticed that the first two squads were selected for guard duty and stationed around this building. I rushed down to find out the meaning of all this. The captain addressed us and explain that thirty-four of us were scheduled to leave for the south. After he called the names from the list I learned that I was not amongst them.

At this point in the diary there is a list of names and addresses (see Appendix III), a list of abbreviations and definitions for apparent memorization (Appendix IV) and a brief list of Mr. Horn's squad members (Appendix V).

Additionally, Mr. Horn did not keep a diary for the remainder of his time at Camp Upton from November 7, 1917 to April 5, 1918. From April 6, 1918 until the end of the war, he was most meticulous about keeping a daily account of his experiences without exception.

Captain Rainsford's account describes a dreary harsh winter of 1917-18 with difficult drilling and training in the snow and mud. There were some breaks in the drudgery:

On a snowy twenty-second of February, 1918 the Division paraded through New York before one of the largest crowds the city had ever gathered, and was greeted with very considerable enthusiasm. Camp Upton was proud of what it had produced, only regretting that it had to court-martial so many of its members immediately thereafter for lack of a proper sense of when the festivities were over.

After this diversion, the mind and spirit of the Camp began to seriously concentrate on the coming departure overseas. That departure from Camp Upton occurred on the morning of April 6. Captain Rainsford writes:

Marched out under arms and packs at 4:15 A.M. Night turning warmer with a dying moon in the east—a silent march through a silent, deserted camp, bringing unexpected regrets of farewell.

This is the end of Volume 1. The adventure now begins in earnest in the following volumes (-ed.)

Volume II

April 6—August 10, 1918

April 6, 1918, Saturday

After lounging around all of yesterday, and spending a very unpleasant night's sleep on our pool table, we were aroused and ordered to form on our company street and prepare to leave at 2 A.M. this morning. Although all was quite (quiet) about us, our hike to the station was made cheerfull {*sic*} by the singing & shouting of our men. We had spent a pleasant stay at Camp Upton but were glad to leave, because things were becoming monotonous. At 3 o'clock we boarded our trains. To us they seemed to be refrigerators. The night was chilly and there was no heat at all in the cars. It was too cold to sleep so we tried to forget our discomfort by singing and whistling. No one knew where we were bound for. Our captain said we were on our way but didn't know where. At 7 A.M. we arrived at Long Island City. We were numb from cold and were glad to get out of those cars. We marched from the train directly to the 34th Ferry. After waiting about 1 ½ hours for the balance of our regiment to board the ferry we started on our way again.

> Got into Long Island City about 7:00 A.M. and ferried around Battery Park to the White Star Docks. Scattered cheering from the other ferries we passed and from a small crowd gathered along the Battery. Our ship, the *Justica*, looks huge, and the officer's quarters as princely as those of the men look crowded and poor.

We were so conjested {*sic*} that one was lucky if he could keep both feet on the deck. Sitting down to rest was out of the question. We were puzzled as to where we were going. We wondered why we had not gone through to the Penn Station. But when the ferry turned south we surmised that we were going around Manhattan Island and board a transport at Hoboken. We passed under the Queensboro[10], Manhattan[11], Williamsburgh[12] & Brooklyn[13] Bridges and gave them a last look of admiration. People were lined along the edge of these bridges and gave us a royal send-off as we passed. As we passed the Statue of Liberty many of the boys remarked that "the old girl sure looks good to us and we darn sorry to leave her". As we turned up the Hudson we could see the inter (?) Dutch Vessels and we were selecting the one on which we would like to sail. We were surprised when we turned towards the N.Y. side and finally landed at pier 59 of the White Star Line[14]. We felt relieved as we marched up the gang plank onto the pier. We had been packed like sardines for about two hours. We formed in a single line and were marched up to the uper {*sic*} teir {*sic*}. Representatives of the Red Cross were on hand and gave each of the boys 2 postal cards which we were to fill out and drop in the mail box. These would be kept by them until cabled news of our safe arrival at our destination was received by them, then they would mail these cards to whom we had addressed them and would bring the good news to them probably a month sooner than we could send it. We were checked up as we boarded the gang plank. I was now on one of the largest transports afloat. She is the Justica[15] recently taken over from Holland by Great Britain. Our company was assigned to C section, which was just above the water line. There were about 50 tables in this section and about 25 men assigned to each table. Hammocks were stretched above the tables and there were racks attached to the ceiling just above the hammocks for more equipment. It was a releif {sic} to unsling our packs. I felt tired and hungry having had nothing since supper last night. I was at table 45, the third table from the pantry (kitchen) and our mess orderlies managed to get well up in line so it was not long before we put on the "feed bag". After mess some of the boys and myself decided to walk about the ship and give her the "once over". We found her to be a boat of tremendous size. At the stern of the boat we saw a big six inch gun. At the bow were two depth bomb guns. We immediately felt at ease to know that we were well protected. We lied down on the top deck of the top deck of the boat and could see some of our boys busily engaged placing our baggage in the hold of the ship. At 5 P.M. we went below for our mess. After mess we began to think of sleep. Where were we going to sleep? "In those hammocks over the tables" said one of our boys. "Ridiculous" we said, how could anyone get onto those things. We were finally convinced that the hammocks were to be our places of rest until we arrived at our destination. I tried to make the best of it and climbed in to sleep. I am so tired I could sleep on a spiked fence. The air is terribly foul. Absolutely no ventilation but you can bet your life I am going to sleep air or no air.

Sunday, April 7, 1918

I was awakened by the command of "Arise Soldiers of the King". I looked out of my hammock in time to see a shoe fly past and hit one of the English stewarts {sic}. He soon learned that we were not, and were darn glad that we weren't Soldiers of the King. While we were at breakfast we felt a slight rocking of the boat. One of the boys looked through the port hole {sic} and informed us that we were just pulling out of the pier. After mess there was a wild scramble to get a last glimpse of N.Y. But in order to make our voyage as secret as possible we were kept below until we were out of sight of land.

> For secrecy, port-holes were painted black, fixed shut, and covered on the inside with zinc shields—which means we can have lights. No one on deck after 8:00 P.M.

Past {sic} the balance of the day lounging about.

Monday, April 8, 1918

Never knew there was so much water in the world. Lounged about all day and sat down when ever we could find room. We are rather crowded. Our ship is carrying about 5,000 troop{sic} & 1000 men of the crew. Sighted land about 8 P.M.

> We sighted Nova Scotia about 5 P.M. and passed the outer lighthouse of Halifax at sunset, anchoring far up in the inner harbor.

We pulled into Halifax Harbor but made no landing. We are anchored and hope we can land to-morrow. I witnessed one of the prettiest Sunsets this evening that I have ever seen. Not long ago a transport carrying dinamite {*sic*} exploded in this harbor. I can see the effects. Houses are ruined as far as I can see. I can see them working on the sunken vessel trying to raise her. I also can see the Belgium Relief ship which colided {*sic*} with her.

> The spires and roofs of Halifax lifted flat and purple against the yellow twilight under an arch of rosy cloud; then the ruins of the lower city swept and crumbled like a village in France; on our port the wreck of the Belgian Relief Ship, half-submerged, the sunset-gilded spruce woods and sandy islands, the quaint old white lighthouse, and the open sea.

Her stern is under water and her bow is high in the air. Retired early to those awful hammocks.

Tuesday, April 9, 1918

Passed a very restless night. Was awakened at 4:30 A.M. by the noise of the mess orderlies forming on line for the eats which will not be served until 7 A.M. Immediately after breakfast I rushed over check to see where we were. We were still in Halifax. I can see the snow in the distance on the mountains. The water about the ship had a thin coat of ice which gradually melted by the heat of the sun.

> A thin skim of glare ice all over the harbor, reflecting in sunshine the screaming flocks of gulls; hoar-frost along the rails and snow over the black, spruce-clad shores. The ocean and city were completely hidden by infolding hills.

It is a beautiful day. We all received our life belts this morning and were instructed to wear them at all times.

Life preservers are never to be left out of reach—
a sort of forewarning of gas masks.

About 10 A.M. we had our first boat drill and were assigned to life boats.

Then we stood for some hours on boat drill. We are told that there is ample accommodation for all in case of accident, but I believe that the swimmers holding to the edge of the rafts are included among those accommodated.

I am assigned to boat 27A. The sea is so calm that some of the life boats {sic} were lowered and the men assigned to them had a sail about the harbor. It was getting too close for dinner for my boat to be lowered so I was deprived of that pleasure. We started upon our journey once more about 5:30 P.M. As we passed through the harbor, two American battle ships that were anchored, turned out their bands to cheer us on our long trip. We cheered each other as we steamed by. It was a wonderful send off.

We weighed anchor about 5 P.M. and pulled out in long succession through the narrow channel—eight transports in column. Women and children gathered in groups along the shore holding out the Stars and Stripes to us; it seemed, too, to fly from the window of every cottage; the crews of the British ships and U.S. man-of-war lined their rails to cheer us as we passed, their bands playing with their whole souls. It was everything we had wanted and missed at New York, and one felt the tingling grip of brotherhood in the great world struggle on which we were launched.

My voice is hoarse from shouting. It gave us all new inspiration & determination to give all we had for the flag which was flying from the ships. Old Glory never looked so good to us before. I am convinced that it is the best looking flag of all nations. Our fleet consists of 8 transports, 1 American Cruiser and one British Auxilary {*sic*} Cruiser.

> **The convoy sailed for the most part in double line under escort of the cruiser *St. Louis*. Little occurred beyond the usual rumors of a sortie by the German fleet—most of who were supposed to have gotten through—or some sudden semaphoring from ship to ship and activity on the part of the *St. Louis*, later explained by the presence of a whale.**

Wednesday April 10
Nothing but water all about us. The sea is pretty rough. The ship is rocking quite a bit and am a little dizzy but not sea sick {*sic*}. My watch is about twenty minutes slow. Upon inquiry of the time I am informed that the clock is set ahead twenty minutes each day so that the difference of 5 hours between English and American time is gradually changed.

Thursday April 11
Physical drill at 9 A.M. Boat drill at 10:30. Balance of the day spent lounging about. Sea not quite as rough as yesterday.

Friday April 12
Sea becoming calmer. Band concert at 1 o'clock by our regiment found and helped to break the monotony. Oh! Where does all this water come from. No other ships but our own in sight.

Saturday April 13

The crew says that they have never experienced such calm weather before. The sea is as smooth as glass. Pysical {*sic*} drill at 8:30. Boat drill 10:30. Band concert at 1 P.M. All must be below decks after 8 P.M. and all lights must be out.

Sunday April 14

Listened to a sermon given by our chaplin {*sic*} which proved interesting. The meals are not as good as they were when we boarded the ship. They are gradually becoming worse. We are getting fish almost every day. No one can eat it. It has a terrible oder {*sic*} and taste and it turns our stomachs. Washing facilities are very poor. The water is turned on at certain hours during the day and it is impossible for us all to wash in such a short period of time. I am compelled to sneak into the officers bath rooms, lock myself in and tend to my wants. Ignore all knocks on the door & answer all questions in a gruff & important tone of voice, but inwardly I pray for the intruder to move on.

Monday April 15

Our gunners had a little practice with the depth bomb guns to see that they were in good condition. A splash and a stream of water like a fountain arise where the bomb strikes. I am informed that these bombs create quite a disturbance in that part of the water where it strikes and nothing is safe within a radius of 300 yds from it.

Tuesday April 16

Same schedule as usual. I check our fleet each morning to make sure all are still with us. We are leading them all because our ship is the fastest of them all. The American Cruiser which is always close to the starboard side of our ship was busily chasing around today. I was told she had sounded a submarine and had chased her away.

Wednesday April 17

At noon we were met by 7 destroyers

> **On the evening of the seventeenth an escort of seven British destroyers appeared, ducking and dodging through the spume like a school of porpoises.**

which brought the total number of vesels {*sic*} in our fleet up to 17. We are now in the danger zone. But look pretty safe with all this protection.

Thursday April 18

On the look out for submarines. Our American Cruiser left us to-day and we certainly feel her loss. No one knows where she went to. She has probably gone on to the American base.

Friday April 19

Sighted land early this morning. Was informed that it was the Irish Coast. As we entered the Irish sea I knew immediately how it received its name. The water was a light green the color of the Irish. Aside from our transports I counted 24 destroyers. Some protection. At 8 P.M. we landed at Liverpool.

> **At dusk of the nineteenth the *Justica* was docked at Liverpool. The troops were disembarked between ten and eleven P.M., and, looking their last on the great ship that loomed above, incredibly vast in the smoky moonlight, were placed directly upon the train for Dover.**

We were delighted to leave the boat, those awful sleeping hammocks and the fish. As we passed down the gang plank {*sic*} we received a days rations, which consisted of a can of bully beef[16], 2 rolls and an orange and an apple. Our company was split into two sections. The other section marched through part of the city. My section en *(entrained?–ed.)* at the station about 100 yards from the pier. The cars are so different from those in the States. They are divided into compartments. Eight of us were put in each compartment. All was dark and little could be seen of the city so we decided to snatch a little sleep as crowded as we were. We have no idea as to where we are going but we are on our way. At about midnight we stopped at Rugby to get some coffee from the Red Cross.

The journey was bitterly cold, and impressions of England were only cheered by the sight of an unusually pretty girl serving coffee during a halt at Rugby about three A.M., and by a clear sunrise over a country white with hoar-frost and cherry blossoms.

But as luck would have it as soon as I was in striking distance on the line, the train began to pull out and we were waved back to our coaches. Not only did I miss the coffee but I was awake from my peaceful slumbers and it was some time before I could fall asleep again.

Saturday, April 20

Spent a very uncomfortable night and awoke about 5 A.M. as the sun came through the window. I got a glimpse of England as we passed through cultivated fields and all seemed clean and orderly. We arrived at Dover

> Arriving at Dover about eight A.M. the troops
> were marched under packs to what appeared to
> be the summit of the highest hill in the neigh-
> borhood for breakfast, and then immediately back
> to the steamer. Nobody liked England; but the
> Channel presented a picture of her grip of the
> seas—wreathed in the smoke of innumerable
> destroyers, above which hovered aeroplanes and
> dirigibles on watch, and somewhere the distant
> firing of guns.

at 8 A.M. It was then that we realized that we were going directly to France. We hiked about 1 mile to an Armory where we were given a hurried breakfast and rushed to the boat which was to take us to France. Two other vessels and about 10 destroyers accampained {sic} us. Our boat contained about 500 men. We were again given life preservers and told we were comming {sic} to the most dangerous part of our voyage. The distance from Dover to Calais is 21 miles across the Straight of Dover. We certainly did speed across to France. Our ship just missed a mine by 20 ft. One of the chasers stopped to fire a machine gun on it and explode it. In a little over an hour we landed at Calais. We hiked about 3 miles to a rest camp No. 6.

> Reaching Calais in the early afternoon of April
> 20, the battalions were marched to different Rest
> Camps and billeted, rather crowdedly, in tents
> sunk a few feet under ground for protection from
> the aerobombs.

On our way we were followed by small children who held out their hands shouting "Souvenir American". We gave them all the small change we had and most of the extra rations we carried. They seemed to be delighted with the white bread we handed them. When we finally arrived at the camp and were assigned to tents, we were so tired that we just lied on the ground and fell asleep until mess time. In the evening some of the boys & myself took a walk to look the town over. We noticed that there were no men under 60 yrs to be seen. They were all serving in the army. The town seemed wrecked by bombs dropped from airoplaines {*sic*}. Houses, churches, & shops were in ruins. Almost every window in town was broken. The people seemed to be suffering of poverty and everywhere as we approached by children asking for "Souvenirs". I entered a house where eats were being served and had the time of my life making myself understood. The folks were very patient & hospitable and a (I) left well satisfied and with a friendly feeling for the French people as a whole. About 11 o'clock I was awakened by loud reports. I soon realized that Fritz[17] was around. Bombs seemed to be dropping almost on top of our tents.

> **Then came the discharge of guns, the soaring scream of projectiles, the occasional soft "thut" of a bullet falling into the sand, and the shock of explosives beyond the canal in the city. From somewhere overhead amid the weaving and crossing searchlights, and the sparkling flash of shrapnel, could be heard the recurrent whirr of German motors.**

I hugged the ground as closely as I could and must admit that I was frightened. Our anti-aircraft guns were firing at the enemys {*sic*} plains {*sic*} and there was an awful noise was wishing it were over and shuddered at the thought of being killed so soon without a chance of getting a crack at the enemy. It lasted about ½ hour and seemed like a week to me. I was real tired and fell asleep as soon as the noise stopped.

Sunday April 21

The first thought that entered my mind when I arose was "Who was hurt from last nights bombardment". I soon learned that the bombs landed about a mile or two from us and into the town. We were in a British camp and were fed by them. We hiked about 3 miles and received our gas masks and gas instructions. Later we received our street helmets, turned in our rifles, boyonets {sic} and amunition {sic} & received British ones instead.

> Two days were spent in fitting and drawing gas-masks, steel helmets, and ammunition, and ex-changing rifles for the British arms.

> It looks as if we will stay with the British, but I sincerely hope they send us to an American base. We had hiked all day from place to place to receive these articles and were real tired when bed time {sic} came. This is the way we spent a restful Sunday in a Rest Camp. I hope there won't be another raid to-night.

Monday April 22

Left our camp at 12 noon. Marched through Calais for about 2 ½ miles to the R.R. Station. Singing and joking all way. The folks turned out to wish us Gods Speed. We could see the effects of the previous nights {sic} bombardment. Received refreshments on the station and were piled into cars marked "8 Chevau{sic} or 40 Hommes" which means 8 horses or 40 men. I had heard of troops traveling in cattle cars but never did I expect to ride in them. No place but the floor to sit and believe me we were packed in worce {sic} than cattle. We rode about 20 miles and saw a few German prisoners working on the roads as we passed.

We traveled from Calais some 20 kilometers to Audriq. From this point the battalions were marched to their different training areas—the First Battalion at Zouafque. The marches were not long, varying from ten to fourteen kilometers, but, as had been anticipated, the packs proved too heavy for all except the strong men. They carried at this time two blankets, half tent with pole and pins, overcoat, slicker, extra boots and underclothes, two days' rations, rifle, bayonet, canteen, and 150 rounds of ammunition, forming a pack which came down to the knees of the smaller men.

We arrived at Audrich[18] and were told to prepare for a six mile hike. Those packs weighing about 80 pounds seemed to weigh 180. After about 2 ½ hours hike we arrived at Zouafques where we were to be billited {sic}. I had imaginations of living with a French family, but when led to a barn with hay on the floor, with 25 other men, my mirage was shattered. The grounds were beautiful. Trees are in full bloom, the lawn is fresh and there is a pond in the centre {sic} of them all. I washed myself & shaved & felt greatly refreshed. After mess I went to sleep and enjoyed my first real nights sleep.

Tuesday, April 23

We were allowed to rest up to-day after all the traveling we did. Beleive {sic} me we needed it. Decided to pitch my tent on the lawn in preference to sleeping with the mice and rats running over my face, in the barn. Retired early.

Wednesday, April 24

The company was rearranged into platoons & squads and I received my permanent squad. Started our schedule of intensive training & drilled hard all day. We had done little work since we left camp & to-day's {*sic*} work effected (affected) us greatly.

April 25 to May 6

During this period we did practically the same thing each day. From 8 A.M. until 5 P.M. we drilled hard to get into shape to fight the Hun. The meals are very poor. We know exactly what to expect for each meal. Breakfast—Bacon—Bread—Coffee Dinner—Stew—Hard tack—supper—cheese, marmalade. Coffee one slice bread. All of these in small portions. Upon making complaints to our officers, we were told that we are attached to the British Forces & are fed by them. These are the rations Tommy gets and fights on. We could not help but remark. "His apperance {*sic*} & fighting qualities shows it". Our officers tried their best to better conditions. They tried to buy food with our company funds but food is very scarce in this section. we bought a cow and a pig but they did not last long. It has rained almost continually since we arrived here. The ground is very muddy and our moral (morale) is very low. We are becomming {*sic*} disgusted with this game. At night "Fritz" pays us an occasional visit to disturb our sleep. It has rained every Sunday since we are here. All I can do is write a few letters and seek shelter for the balance of the day. It is about 15 minutes walk to the village from our billets. We can buy souvenirs and drinks. We try to buy food but it is difficult to get it.

Tuesday May 7

Walked about two miles for a bath but it was worth the trouble. It is the first we got since we arrived here. The water is pumped from a stream into a boiler where it is heated and passes through pipes and through showers. Its {*sic*} a queer looking affair but it answers the purpose and I feel greatly refreshed. The only water facilities we have at our billets is the pond. We wash in it in the morning. Clean our mess kits and clothes in it and shave in it. Water to drink is brought to us from wells in water carts. This evening we hiked to our Battalion Drill Fields about 3 miles away to receive gas instruction. We entered our training trenches and had real chlorine gas sent at us. The alarm was given and we had to put our masks on hurriedly. The attack lasted about twenty minutes. One breath would have been enough to kill you. No one was injured. It was 11:30 before we returned to our billets and I was real tired.

Wednesday May 8

Reviewed by high officials of the British & American Forces while at the Target range. Drill as usual.

> The lack of adequate training ground was keenly felt, and the French in this region were far from generous in making such available. Yet thirty yard rifle ranges with reduced targets were improvised.

Thursday May 9

Witnessed an air battle between 2 German & 5 Allied planes. Germans were finally driven away. Drill as usual.

Friday May 10

Was selected to attend the auto-rifle school in charge of seven men which constitute a machine-gun squad. Spent the day watching other Lewis Guners [19]{*sic*} at work.

> The Lewis Gun teams, four to each platoon, picked from the best material, took hold of their work with genuine enthusiasm, evincing the first real *esprit de corps* to be developed.

Saturday May 11

Busy studying the mechanism of the Lewis Gun. Paid this evening. Received 111 Francs. Sounds like real money, Doesn't it? Informed that reveille would be at 4:30 to-morrow . To make preparations to hike about 6 miles to the rifle range. It's a shame to select Sunday for some work.

Sunday May 12

Reveille sounded at 6:30 A.M. Was surprised to learn that the hike had to be called off. To-day is Mother's Day. We celebrated by writing a letter to home. I make it a habit to write home every Sunday anyhow. At noon we were ordered to turn in our extra clothing & one blanket. Our personal articles were put in our Blue Barrack Bags. Were told we wouldn't see them before the duration of the war. We were instructed to be prepared to move within an hour's notice, so I got busy making my pack. Spent the balance of the day waiting to go, we knew not where (*Audriq–ed.*). Lied down in the barn to get a little rest. Sleep disturbed about 2 A.M. by another air raid. Barn and surrounding ground trembled. Windows smashed.

Monday May 13

After spending a very unrestfull night, awoke at 6 A.M. chilled to the bone. Received our iron rations about 11 A.M. Was informed we would move at 9 P.M. Slep {sic} in the afternoon. Formed at 8:30 P.M. with packs. Before we left the captain thanked the folks at the Chateau{sic} for their courtesies and spoke a few words to us. He held up, in his arms, one of the children of the family and said "Men we are fighting for the preservation of these children of France & for the children of the U.S.A. We will prevent the Hun from continuing to massicre {sic} these inocent {sic} children & I know you will all make a good showing. Let us give three cheers for the children of France & U.S.A." We gave them with great enthusiasm. We also cheered our Captain & Officers. Then we started on our hike back to Aurdrick[20] singing the "Marcelois" [21]. We marched in a down pour of rain and were dripping wet when we arrived about midnight.

After three weeks of almost daily rain, the battalions marched again to Audriq, where they took a train to Mondicourt. Here they were to be brigaded for training, and it was thought also for combat, with different battalions of Manchester and East Lancashire troops, of the Forty-second British division. The First battalion was brigaded at Couin.

May 14, Tuesday

Spent a very uncomfortable night in these cattle cars. About 50 men were crowded in my car. I was compelled to sleep in a sitting position with my knees under my chin. I feel ill. I have pains & chills throughout my body. Arrived at Monte Court-Pas Station [22] at 2:30 P.M. Received some hot cocoa but felt a fever comming {*sic*} over me. Started for our camp at 3 P.M. with full packs led by an English Band.

> Somewhere in the darkness ahead, a British band was playing the troops magnificently in. They know how to use their music, the British, and it seemed strange that the regiment should leave America in the silence of the plague-stricken, to be escorted into the forward area with a brass band. *(Although when they left new York there were some cheering people, as recorded above, the soldiers were deeply resentful that there was not even a band or any official pomp to acknowledge there departure.—ed.)*

Hiked about six miles up a steep incline and seemed as if I was in a trance. Encamped at Couin[23] and was assigned to a tent. With the aid of some of my comrades I undress and went to sleep on the hard earth.

Wednesday May 15

Rested fairly well last night. Awakened occasionally by the roar of the cannon which is located only ½ mile in front of us. Fritz was over several times this morning but was driven back each time. Stayed in my bunk all day. The doctor gave me some pills and medicine.

Thursday May 16

Remained in my bunk all day. Feel much better except for a terrific headache. The boys tell me there is a scarcity of water here. The water cart brings water only once a day, allowing us only a cateenful {*sic*}. We must filter our water, to wash with, from a well about ½ mile away. The cannons have roared all day. Air fights are a common occurrence.

Friday May 17

Left my bunk to-day. Feel O.K. but a trifle weak. To notice for the first time as to where I was. Our camp is situated on a high hill in the midst of a woods.

> The country was beautiful, the weather immaculate, the training systematic and efficient. Save for the infrequent passage or seemingly unaimed arrival of a shell in the beautiful wheat fields, or the more frequent and important shortage of rations, there was little to mar the tranquility of the summer days. The troops were quartered in large conical or small shelter tents, as the case may be, along the edge of the splendid beechwoods.

Two of our observation balloons are visible. Took things easy today. Did not drill with the company. Had my hair clipped this evening. Am an awful sight. I'd give anything to have my hair back again. Attended an entertainment given by some of the boys of my battalion.

> The British Tommies of the battalion gave an open-air vaudeville performances in costume every week, at which all American troops were welcome.

Good show.

Saturday May 18

Feeling fairly well. Attended school for instructions on the Lewis Gun. Big shells from the German Artillery could be heard wizzing {*sic*} over our heads going in the direction of

Pas[24]. Big artillery duel at night. Don't mind it so much now and am able to go to sleep through most of it.

Sunday May 19

The first pleasant Sunday since I am in France. Visited the town of Pas which is about 3 ½ miles from camp. Most of the inhabitants have evacuated the town. There is nothing of interest there. Ate some eggs and potatoes and drank some wine. Bought some things to eat and returned tired. Usual heavy firing at night.

Monday May 20

Attended school. Received a letter forwarded from camp Upton—And it helped immensely to cheer me up. Heavy barrage bombardment all night.

Tuesday May 21

Attended school. Forgot to mention that it is under the supervision of an English officer.

Captain Illingworth, an English officer of the 16th Sherwood Foresters, with his staff of specialist N.C.O.'s, was assigned temporarily to the regiment to assist in the instruction of the troops

We are attached to the British Forces. The 42nd Division. We are held in reserve. Should the Germans break through at this point, we will have to occupy the reserve trenches and do our bit to stem the tide.

(In trench warfare, each side almost always had at least two trench lines for defense. The first, which was deeply dug and heavily

fortified with barbed wire and large numbers of troops, was considered the "frontline". The second, or reserve, trench line was usually located a mile or more behind the first and was a more relaxed place where men were kept in reserve. Should the frontline collapse, it would be the duty of these soldiers to stem the onslaught of enemy forces. As will be seen later, the reserve troops would rotate with the frontline troops as relief.

Later in the war, especially at the more contested areas of the front across France, the Germans created a third line behind the second. This made possible the German tactic of lightly manning the frontline trench allowing the allied forces to seemingly achieve a breakthrough. The second trench line was really where all the German soldiers and machine guns were waiting behind deep barbed wire barricades. This ploy would cause tremendous loss of life as it was very difficult for the soldiers to effectively retreat because of the obstacle the first trench posed. The German artillery was also poised to strike the area between the first and second trench line therefore contributing to an even greater number of casualties.

This tactic allowed the Germans to leave a contested area lightly guarded and move the reserve troops to where they were more needed. The allied soldiers could never be sure if the lightly defended frontline trenches were a true opportunity for a breakthrough or another deadly trap.–ed.)

Wednesday May 22

Pretty warm to-day. Our platoon marched down for a bath. Feel fine & clean once again. The firing has quieted down a bit.

Thursday May 23

Had the pleasure of firing a Lewis Gun this morning. Quiet all day. Visited the place from which one of the balloons rise, this evening. The aviators in charge were very courteous & explain everything to us. They also showed us a few shell holes caused by the German bombardment the other night. Got a good night's sleep.

Friday, May 24

Very cloudy morning. Hiked to the target range about 2 miles from camp. It rained so hard that we had to return. Walked all the way back with our gas masks on. It was very uncomfortable. By the way, we must carry our gas masks with us at all times, just as we did the life preservers on the boat. It continues to rain all day. Retired at 7 P.M. to give my clothes an opportunity to dry.

Saturday, May 25

Drilled all day. Went on Battalion Guard at 6 P.M. which last for 24 hours. I am corporal of the first relief. Heavy bombardment started about 10 P.M. The sky was illuminated by the flashes of the big guns. Saw flashes in the woods. Took one of the guards with me to investigate. Proved to be some soldiers under the influence of liquor trying to find their quarters. Made them extinguish their lights as a precaution from being observed by evening planes.

Sunday May 26

Saw prisoners captured in a raid last night. They were taken to the intelligence dep't {sic}to gain information. By their actions they seemed pleased to be captured. They were rather young and filthy with dirt. We were ordered to dig two feet beneath our tents and reinforce the sides with dirt, as a protection from bursting shells. Retired early.

Monday May 27

Drill as usual. "Fritz" made an attempt to get our balloon. The occupants jumped down in parachutes. He failed in his attempt and was driven off by our 'planes. An order was issued compelling us to wear our gas masks ½ hour back in the morning & afternoon as to become accustomed to it. We dread those moments because the mask is very uncomfortable.

Tuesday May 28

Drill as usual. Retired early.

Wednesday May 29

Another bath! What do you think of that. Drill as usual.

Thursday May 30

Surprised when ordered out for drill. We expected a holiday. To-day being Decoration Day[25]. Hiked to our rifle range and watched the British in maneuvers. Then took a few shots at some tin cans. Returned at 2:30 P.M. Had our dinner and rested the balance of the day. At retreat we were informed that the order declaring to-day a holiday had been delayed and that we would be off to-morrow instead. Signed the payroll this evening.

May 31, Friday

All inhabitants still remaining in the village were ordered to move as the town expected to be bombarded. "Mustered in" at 4:30. Heavy firing all night. Had expected to be reviewed by Gen. Pershing so to-day's holiday was postponed until to-morrow.

Saturday June 1

Field inspection this morning. Rested the balance of the day. Heard that one of our boys had died in the hospital from Spinelmengitis[26] {sic}.

Sunday June 2

Spent a quiet day. Visited the cemetery near our camp and watched them bury a few English soldiers. They are sown (sewn) in a blanket and placed sometimes three & more in one grave. Saw a new plot marked "American Plot". This was reserved for our battalion and it gave me the shivers to think of having some of my chums buried there. Was told we were to go on an overnight hike to-morrow so we rested all day and retired early.

Monday June 3

Arose & 5 A.M. & got in the job preparing for the hike left at 7:30. Walked 2 ½ miles, pitched tents & rested all morning. Our platoon built a shell proof dug-out in the afternoon. At 7:30 P.M. we filed into our training trenches and imagined we were holding them against the Hun. Several aeroplanes passed close to us and I assure they are brutal looking things. They appear to be swift flying monsters. We were relieved by Co. B. at 10:30 P.M. and went back to our tents to sleep. The night was very chilly and only once did I feel as cold before and that was my first night at Upton.

Tuesday June 4

Awakened at 5 A.M. Hiked 3 ½ miles to an open field, with trenches and fought a sham battle. Returned to temporary camp, eat and broke camp. Moved back to our camp at 2:45. We have hiked 10 miles to-day with our packs. One of our sergeants took sick on the hike home. I dropped out with him & carried his pack in addition to my own. This evening we were told we were to move to a Southern camp. We hope it is the American base. Am on guard to-night.

Wednesday June 5

Celebrated this day the anniversary of Registration Day[27], with a bath. English troops were just finishing bathing & were having a cootie hunt. I hesitated to bathe after them fearing I might catch them. Saw the big 9.2 naval gun on the R.R. tracks, all camouflaged and cursed it for depriving me of so much sleep by its loud reports at night.

Thursday June 6

Received notice to prepare to move. Busy all morning leveling the ground and cleaning up. We always leave a place in the best possible condition. Left at 2:30 loaded down with heavy pack & overcoat. English band turned out and gave us a send off. Hiked to Pas. Stacked arms, turned in our British rifles & amunition {*sic*}.

> All British equipment was ordered turned in, including rifles and the now beloved Lewis guns, and the regiment marched west. The sudden-

ness of this equipment change at the moment of coming action was mortifying in the extreme, for it seemed almost like desertion in the face of the enemy. There might well have been a little jeering from the British, but there was none. Instead, to their honor be it said, a British band, hurriedly assembled, played them out upon their way.

Also our overcoats. Am under the impression we are headed for the American Base. We all feel happy to leave the English. There is no love lost between them & us.

If only the men could have learned to like the British ration, British shoes, and the British Tommy, we might all have been perfectly happy. But the first was too short, the second too flat, and the trouble with the last rather difficult to determine. Unfortunately the American soldier, probably harking back to the injurious history books of school-days, decided to hate him; yet the feeling does not seem to have been reciprocal, and nothing could have exceeded the hospitality, courtesy, and welcoming, painstaking kindness of the British officers.

Ate supper and continued our hike at 7:30. Hiked all night and arrived at Cezan Court [28] at 11:30 P.M. Billited {*sic*} in an old barn & went to sleep on the hard earth. Total distance hiked to-day is 13 ¼ miles.

A four day march was made to the entraining points at Longpré and Saint Remy. The First battalion halting at Gezaincourt, Bernaville, and Ailly-le-Haut-Clocher. Only the first day's march was severe, some twenty-four kilometers, at the end of which rifles and ammunition were issued from trucks.

Friday June 7

Rested all morning. Resumed our march at 2:30 P.M. Stopped at a field about 5 ¾ miles further on. Received American Rifles, bayonets & amunition {sic}. Ate lunch and rested until 5 P.M. Continued again to Bernsville[29] 3 miles on and {sic} in barns again. Washed my face, hands & feet also shaved. Felt greatly releieved {sic}. Retired early.

Saturday, June 8

Slept well last night. Our morning rations had not come up yet so we had to be content with bread & jam for breakfast. Resumed our hike at 8:30 A.M. Stopped after walking 6 ¾ miles, in a field for lunch. A few of the boys were complaining of swollen feet & blisters. The big majority including myself felt fine. Hiked 4 ¾ miles more. Came to the village of Ally L' Ht Clocher [30] and were assigned to barns. They were so filthy that most of the boys decided to pitch tents for the night. To keep up the good spirit amongst the men, the captain gave us a blow out. He purchased 150 bottles of wine, which was readily consumed by the company. Feeling frisky & gay retired to my dog-tent for a good snooze.

Sunday, June 9

Rested all morning. Continued with our hike at 1 o'clock. All through this hike we were seeing a great deal of France and were greatly impressed by her beauty.

The wide valley of the Somme, with its intricate maze of canals and lagoons glittering in sunshine

through the foliage of innumerable lines of poplars, was a picture to cherish.

Passed a few airdromes[31] and many British & New Zealand troops. We were cheered all along our march. Hiked 6 ½ miles to Port Remy[32] the end of the hike. Total number of miles hiked on trip is exactly 40 miles. We entrained imediately {*sic*} in those "40 Hommes or 8 Chevaux" Pullmans. We are a little more comfortable on this trip. We have 29 men in our car. Stole some hay from another train and got busy making our car as comfortable as we could. Pulled out of the station at 5:30 P.M.

The journey by train led west and south, skirting Paris, then southeast to the Moselle, where the regiment was detrained at Chatel and Thaon on the night of June eleventh. Save for the cold of the nights and the inevitable discomfort of the cattle cars, it was a memorable journey.

We are on our way but we don't know where we are going. Passed through Armiens[33] late in the evening. The town is deserted except for a few troops. It has been heavily bombarded these last few days and is entirely in ruins. It seems as if the inhabitants rushed from the place leaving everything as it was. In some places tables were set with dishes and remained that way.

Monday, June 10

Slept well last night. Rained all of last night and slight drizzling now. Stopped at Chars for twenty-five minutes. Washed in a nearby spring and had breakfast. Passed around the outskirts of Paris, but could see very little of the city. Stopped at St. George[34] for lunch, supper was served at 3:30 so that we could continue through until morning without stopping. Were cheered all along the way by the French people. They threw flowers at us and some were waving the American Flag as we passed.

> The civilian population of every town flocked to windows and gardens to wave and cheer to "les Américains"; at every halt the loveliest in the land seemed to have been gathered to give out coffee and flowers along the station platforms; and at one momentary stop outside a tunnel a particularly sweet-looking French girl was found, by chance or otherwise, picking flowers besides the track. Having been kissed by one soldier, she continued generously along the length of the train, showing little or no favoritism, and, as the train moved on through the tunnel, her figure in black silhouette against the diminishing arch of sunshine, kissing her hand again and again into the darkness, left a picture such as is good for fighting men to carry with them.

It was a wonderful sight and brought great joy to our hearts. Gazed upon the beautiful passing senery {sic} until dark. Then packed ourselves in sardine fashion and slept.

Tuesday June 11

Stopped at Wassy[35] for a hurried breakfast. Admired the country and cheered and were cheered by the French people and soldiers that we passed. Stopped at Toul at 2 P.M. for lunch. Was met by some of the American Red Cross and served with cocoa & tobacco. Gee but its great to meet a girl from your home country. We did not stay long and left with lingering glances at the girls. American troops could be seen scattered about this sector and we were glad to be rid of the

English and get in with some regular fellows. Passed through the city of Nancy. It is the bigest {sic} town we have seen in France. It is a very pretty place and I was wishing we would stop near there. Arrived at Thoan[36] where we got off the train at 7:30 P.M. Although we are tired we were notified that our company was detailed to handle the baggage of our regiment. We stayed up all night unloading the trains as they came in and loading the baggage on lories.

Wednesday June 12

Rested all morning. Looked the town over. It is the largest aside of Calais that we have stopped at. Were informed we are due for another hike. Left at 4 P.M. and hiked 11 miles to the village of Gier Court[37]. Arrived there at 8:30 P.M.

> **Detraining did not occur until towards midnight, the battalions moved, the First to Longchamps and Giercourt, the Second to Bult, the Third to Sercoer and Dompierre.**

Ate supper and were billited {sic} in barns. Plenty of hay around. Made a soft bed a {sic} prepared for a good sleep.

P.S. To prove the affection of the French people towards us. A few French girls followed our company from Thoan on bicycles.

Thursday June 13

Slept like a log last night. Rested all morning & cleaned my clothes & equipment. Field inspection in the afternoon. Our billets in the barns were found to be unsanitary so the entire company pitched tents in a nearby pasture.

We had the men pitch their half-tents in the flat meadows along the stream. The next morning was spent riding about looking for drill-grounds, as we expected to be here a week, and then called on the mayor. I told him that in order to beat the Boche the men had to be drilled and trained, and that the only available ground seemed to be the recently harvested hay meadows along the bottom of the valley, though this would rather interfere with their growing a second crop. He said they were community meadows, and if I thought them necessary for drilling the troops that was probably a better use to put them to than growing hay; after all, we were at war, and the village did not want to be paid for them

We start are {sic} schedule of drill to-morrow so am retiring early.

Friday June 14
Drilled all day.

Saturday June 15
A cup of coffee was all we had for breakfast. This had to furnish all the energy & strength for the morning's drill. Rained in the afternoon while we were at the parade grounds and came back drenched to the skin. Was excused for the balance of the day to allow my equipment to dry.

Sunday June 16
No drills to-day. Three of the boys & myself took a hike to Rambersville[38] which is 12 K. from our camp. It is a big town & many things could be purchased. We arrived in town

at 1:03 P.M. Just 3 minutes to {*sic*} late to get anything to eat. Found an American YMCA & made a few purchases. Looked the town over & started on our return at 2:30 P.M. My friend had a pedometer and it registered 25 miles walking for the day. Retired early.

Monday June 17

On prison guard for 12 hours. Raining & gloomy. Ordered to prepare to move. Received my automatic revolver & trench knife. Started from camp at 8 P.M. Hiked all night, passing through Rambersville. Slight drizzle & pitch dark. Was unable to distinguish anyone near you. Arrived at Menil[39] after hiking about 15 miles, at 2:30 A.M.

> **On June seventeenth, the First Battalion moved to the ruined hamlet of Mesnil, the high water mark of the German invasion of 1914.**

The billets we were to occupy were filled with French troops,

> **Through the gaunt ruins and moon-blanched streets of Mesnil our black column wound its way. Toward midnight we billeted on a hilltop overlooking Baccarat in barns already crowded with troops who were supposed to have left.**

so we were compelled to sleep in the wet grass of a nearby pasture.

Tuesday June 18

Rested all day. Resumed our march at 8 P.M. Passed the 165th Regiment (Old 69th) as they were coming from the

trenches. It is rumored that we will receive them. Hiked until 2:30 A.M. after covering 15 miles. Waited about, until 4
A.M. until billets were found for us. I am so tired I can sleep
on a spiked fence. Am in the village of Vacquesville about 7
miles from the front.

> **Thence, the next evening, we moved on to
> Vaqueville, a dirty and inhospitable little village
> close behind the rather ill-defined Line of Re-
> sistance.**

Passed through Baccarat[40] on our way here. Town is in
ruins from bombardment.

Wednesday June 19

Slept until 11 A.M. Ate our breakfast & dinner to-gether
{*sic*} at 1 P.M. It is rumored that 70 men of the 308th were
gassed last night. Rested all afternoon. Am preparing to leave,
at 7:30 P.M., with the rest of the N.C.O's. of the company, for
the front line trenches. Left at 9 P.M. Marched about 2 miles
when it began to rain in torrents. Walked about 15 minutes
before we could get shelter in a ruined barn. It proved nothing more than a shower and resumed the march after 15 minutes, drenched through & through. Passed through gaps in
the barbed wire & saw shell holes all about us. Arrived at St.
Maurice[41] about 12:30 A.M. The trenches are directly out of
the village. We were led by French guides to the sector we
were to hold. Were mixed in with some lads from Alabama
N.G. and shared their bunks with them while they went on
guard.

> **The next evening we marched through the town
> against the turbulent counter-current of the
> Forty-second's Alabamans, a splendid-looking lot**

of men, who appeared only by chance to be wearing uniforms.

Our company will relieve them to-morrow night and then
the French & ourselves will hold these trenches.

**On the twentieth, Battalion Headquarters moved
up to St. Maurice, with companies D and A on
the frontline at Neuviller. We will relieve the
forward elements of the Forty-second Division
on the front line during the night of the twenty-
first.**

The night was very chilly & slept very little. Heard the
artillery in action & the shells whistling overhead. We have
the distinction of being the first company of the N.A.[42] to
enter the trenches.

Thursday, June 20

Rested & snatched a bit of sleep in the dug outs, during
the day. Found some amusement in watching the rats run
around. They are as large as cats. Rained all day making the
ground wet & muddy. Aside of a few shells from our artillery
screeching over our heads, things were very quite {*sic*}. Our
company joined us about midnight and relieved the 167th.
Awakened about 3 A.M. and "stood alert". At sundown &
sunrise is the time an attack is to be expected. Therefore at
those times we stand alert until it is either dark or daylight.

Friday, June 21

Slept all morning. It has rained all last night and the ground
is in terrible condition. Am ankle deep in mud. Can't move
without slipping.

> With the darkness came the rain, at first a few
> large drops and then a roaring cloudburst. The
> evening had started and the raincoats were
> stowed inside the packs, where they alone re-
> mained dry. Then the rain ceased and moonlight
> flooded the dark sprucewood, lighting mysteri-
> ous vistas in its wet and misty depths.

Explored our platoon's area. Seems like a Chinese puzzel
{sic}. Only excitement to-day occurred at evening mess. We
crowd around the food, having had little to eat the previous
meals, when a shell came screeching close over our heads.
We scrambled in all directions. I immediately fell flat on the
ground, covered with mud until I was assured all was safe. I
spilled a portion of the beans, which constituted the meal
and got back to my dugout. The shrapnel bursted about 50
yds from us. No one was injured. The sun & rain played tag
all day. Stood alert from 8 P.M. to 9:30 P.M.

Saturday June 22
Stood alert from 3 to 4:30 A.M. in a heavy rain. We will
soon be able to swim if this rain continues. One slice of bread
& coffee for breakfast. The meals are very poor since we
took over these trenches and the boys all complain. Am corporal of the guard to-day. Sun shone this afternoon hope it
stays out for the balance of our stay here. Heavy bombardment of German lines by our artillery. Germans are very quiet.
Retired after standing alert.

Sunday June 23
Fairly quiet all day. Went out with a patrol 9 P.M. returned
11 P.M. Germans tampering with our barbed wire about midnight & drew our machine guns fire.

Monday June 24

Just reached my post at 3 A.M. when the sky seemed to open and shells were screeming {*sic*} over our heads.

> About three A.M. of the twenty-forth, a single shell came wailing in and exploded near the church; two more followed and then the storm burst. The shelling was heavily mixed with gas. The men ducked to the nearest shelter and waited; they waited too long and would have been better if they had never ducked at all. A number were caught in the dugouts and shelters, bombed or burned to death.

Got busy distributing bombs to our men and waited for something to happen. The shells were comming {*sic*} thick & furious. Shrapnel was bursting all about us. It seemed as if heaven & earth had cut loose. About 6 A.M. 7 men & myself were sent to the trench ahead to help the 3rd platoon. Took charge of their ammunition. Barraged quieted down about 6:30 and returned to my platoon. Just as I got to my dugout one of the men asked for someone to help carry the wounded to the dressing station. It was then I realized that great damage had been done. The first man I helped to carry was a man from my own squad. He had nine shrapnel wounds. Saw quite a few of my friends brought in as I waited around. Learned that the Boshe[43]{*sic*} had come over and attacked our flank They certainly tried hard to entertain us. They gave us all they had and showed us all they knew. They put up a good show. We had shrapnel & gas shells coming over. Five of their airplanes were busy supervising the attack and flying very low at times firing their machine guns into the trenches at us.

Their contact planes were especially active right above us, and I counted six at one time. We were forced to lie then in the trenches and wait.

The sectors which they attacked were held by our 1st & 2nd platoons. They came over in mass formation shooting machine guns & liquid fire at our men.

There was hoarse shouting in the darkness and then the Germans attacked. They attacked with rifles, hand grenades, light machine guns strapped to their backs, heavy machine guns from low flying aeroplanes, aeroplane bombs, and with flame throwers. A confused fight took place in the gray of dawn through the dense smoke of the echoing ruins. The French, for the most part, had withdrawn at the first opportunity; the Americans, broken into scattered groups amidst the maze of trenches, wire hurdles, and barricades fought their best.

Their forces were far superior in number and our men were forced to retire. They were followed by men throwing bombs and liquid fire. Our wounded and dead were stabbed with bayonets to be sure they were dead. The report I received was that our casualties were about 50.

At daylight the company, with some French troops, attempted to counter-attack, but found the battle ground deserted, the Germans having, however, taken the time to rifle and destroy the stores of the Company D kitchen and to remove their own casualties. One German, a sergeant, found shot dead in the central square, and another transfixed by a French bayonet in the barbed wire were all that remained. Company D reckoned seven killed, twenty-five wounded and three missing; Company C, one killed and two wounded from artillery fire; while Company B, working through the ensuing day about the shell holes had seventy men gassed to death.

The Germans carried their wounded and dead back with them so we are not certain of their losses but it is estimated that they are greater than ours.

Of the number of enemy engaged in the *coup-de-main* no fair estimate can be formed, though information from American prisoners, taken at this time and returned after the armistice, fairly indicates that a special force was brought from elsewhere for the attack, departing by train the next day, and that their losses, incurred for the most part by machine-gun fire during their withdrawal, were quite unexpectedly heavy.

The section held by the 3rd & 4th platoon (I am in the 4th) succeeded in keeping the enemy away and suffered no losses at all. This is the first time since the beginning of the war that so big an attack was made in this sector. We all feel upset about it and vow vengeance. Our kitchen was shot to ruins and the little food we received to-day was furnished us by other companies.

One man of Company D, whose discretion had never been questioned, spent the entire period of enemy occupation beneath the company rolling kitchen, maintaining a strategic silence while the kitchen stores were being looted, and even while the kitchen itself was being blown up with grenades. He emerged to greet the counter-attacking troops of company A, and seemed to claim a certain distinction at not having been driven from his post by the whole of the Hindenberg Circus, which he had faced (?) single-handed.

Tuesday June 25

Was awakened at 2 A.M. to go out on a patrol.

During this time there had been little or no activity beyond nightly patrols into the vast desert of No Man's Land, where enemy patrols were seldom encountered, and never at close range, and where the principle danger faced was from the somewhat nervous fire from both French and American outposts. Patrols occasionally penetrated the enemy lines, in search of prisoners, but without encountering resistance. They were usually ordered so to penetrate and reported having done so—in good faith but often with doubtful accuracy, for in that labyrinth of old wire, crumbling trenches, unmapped trails and willow thickets it was difficult in the darkness to be sure of position.

Our party consisted of 8 Americans & 2 French. We made the round of our entire sector, visiting Neuvillar[44] were {sic} the fighting took place yesterday.

Neuviller, a tiny ruined village on an isolated hill, that must once have been a very pleasant little spot, and is still, though more grimly, picturesque,

**with its loopholed cobblestone barricades, stood
out as a dangerous salient from the French lines.**

The place is entirely in ruins from the heavy bombardment. Witnessed some of our dead being brought through
the trenches. Returned at 4 A.M. Went to sleep at 5:30 A.M.
Have had very little sleep these last few days and am nearly
exhausted. Aside from a few shells from our artillery, things
were fairly quiet. Took advantage of this and had a much
needed rest. Prepared to move into the reserves late in the
afternoon. Did move until about 10:30 P.M. Was assigned to
our sector about midnight. These are partly constructed
trenches with no dugouts in which to sleep. The men made
themselves as comfortable as possible. Some sleeping at the
bottom of the trenches. Others sleeping on the earth at the
brink of the trenches. I am corporal of the guard and stayed
awake all night.

Wednesday June 26

After breakfast I pitched my tent close to the trenches
and camouflaged it with twigs & leaves. Slept all morning.
After dinner I read my shirt and engadged {*sic*} in a cootie
hunt. After which I lied down for a nap. I was placed in charge
of the autorifles of my section. Fairly quiet. Retired early but
night was very chilly and rested uneasy.

Thursday June 27

Rested most of the day, being corporal of the guard. Was
informed that I was selected to attend school with 10 other
men of the company, for instruction in the use of the auto-
rifles. Left the trenches at 6:30 P.M. passing through the village of St. Maurice where our reserves are quartered. Every
house is ruined from shell fire. Arrived at Vacqueville at 10:30
and was billited {*sic*} for the night.

Friday June 28

Arose 6 A.M. After breakfast hiked to Indian Village[45] took Lorie for Moyen[46]. Where we will study the mechanism of the Chanshot[47] Rifle. Rested the balance of the day.

On the night of June twenty-eighth, the Second Battalion took over the line, the Third battalion moving to Vacqueville, and the First Battalion to Haxo Barracks in Baccarat.

Saturday, June 29

Studied mechanism of rifle this morning. Shot on the range this afternoon. Like this place very well. Seems like a vacation after comming {*sic*} out of the line.

The region about and behind the front was of vast woodlands alternating with open and dusty meadows. In places the woods had been blown to pieces with artillery fire, and in places the meadows were pitted with craters of sun-cracked clay. One particular stretch of open marsh, near some abandoned artillery emplacements on the Line of Resistance, had been churned up into something like the surface of a sponge, and still, on misty nights, reeked with the sickish acid smell of gas.

Invited some Frenchmen in our billets this evening and had a sociable time. There were about 15 in the party. We opened plenty of beer & wine, sang & told stories. Retired about 10:30 P.M.

Sunday June 30

Arose 5 A.M. From 6:30 to 9 A.M. I studied mechanism of rifle. Shot on the range in the afternoon. Retired early.

Monday July 1

Same schedule as yesterday.

Tuesday July 2

Same as yesterday.

Wednesday July 3

Studied in the morning. Cleaned our training equipment and turned them in afternoon. Started to celebrate the 4th this evening by opening a few cases of beer. Retired feeling pretty gay & happy.

Thursday July 4

Was permited {sic} to sleep until 7:30 A.M. The boys who represented our company (11 strong) had 3 large pies baked by a French family. We invited 3 of our French comrades, who joined us about 2 P.M. They brought 2 loaves of French bread, jam, nuts & prunes. All this together with some vin rouge furnished quite a spread and believe me we had some party. At 8 P.M. we had a concert & entertainment. There was both French & American talent on the program. The show proved very entertaining and was enjoyed by all present. After the show we listened to speaches {sic} by the Major, the French Colonel and some of our officers. Then the fireworks started and some of the boys shot their rifles & revolvers into the air. French & American soldiers & officers intermingled freely. All joined hands and danced around in circles, shouting & singing. We acted like a bunch of kids but it was the only way we could show our affection towards each other. Finally we formed in marching order French & American arm in arm. We paraded through all the streets in town, and I assure you, we made some racket. Disbanded about midnight with shouts of "Viva la France", "Viva la Amérique".

Friday July 5

The officer in charge of our outfit overslept, so drills were called off for the day. He probably had not got over the effects of yesterday's celebration. Rolled our packs this afternoon ready to leave and join our company. Piled into lories about 9 P.M. and were given a send off by our French comrades. Rode about 4 hours evidently got lost on the way and were led to the building in which our company is billeted. Could find no sleeping quarters so prepared to sleep on the concrete floor in the hall overnight.

Saturday July 6

The first thing I did after breakfast was to look up the captain and report back to duty. Also told him I was sadly in need of a bath, that I was broke and needed money, and that I wanted my mail. He saw to it that I got all I wanted. Felt fine after my hot bath & change of clothes. Received a big batch of letters and spent the balance of the morning reading same & answering them. Strolled around town in the afternoon and spent some of my doe {sic}. Saw a show given by our divisional troop. It was a riot, the best I have seen in France. Had found better sleeping quarters and retired after the performance.

Sunday July 7

Rested & wrote letters all day. Retired early to my cot consisting of three boards stretched over two iron supports.

Monday July 8

On July eighth the Third Battalion took the front while the First and Second remained back as reserves.

Had charge of a detail to police the streets around the barracks. Spent the balance of the morning writing letters. Rested in the afternoon and rolled my pack to be ready to move to-night. Left at 8 P.M. and arrived at Vacaqueville at 11 P.M. Were billited {*sic*} in barns and prepared for a night's sleep with my friends the rat & cooties.

Tuesday July 9

Rested all day.

Wednesday July 10

Rested during the morning. Had a little target practice in the afternoon. Went on Batt Guard at 5 P.M. Rained in torrents during my first shift. The night is dark and have difficulty finding my posts. Clearing about 12 M.

Thursday July 11

Was relieved from guard duty about 10 A.M. to attend school and receive instructions in observation. School meets at Batt. Hdqtrs. Elsie Janis[48] payed {*sic*} us a visit at the YMCA

Hut at 1 P.M. Enjoyed her company. We all agreed that she is wonderful. Attended school again after performance.

Friday July 12

Attended school in the morning. Went out to the target range in the P.M. and shot my rifle & revolver. Practicing up for the Boshe. Rolled my pack & left my billet about 9 P.M. to relieve 2 of our platoons who are acting as reserves in the woods. While we were marching across an open field our Lieutenant had us gather around him. He informed us that some of the men of our division were going over the top to-night and that our artillery would probably be very active. We were cautioned to be on the alert for gas which the Germans would most likely send over to retaliate. When we arrived at our destination most of the men were assigned to posts for guard duty. I was fortunate enough not to be selected, so I pitched my tent in the dark and rolled in to sleep.

Saturday July 13

Awoke at 5 A.M. Inquired about last night's attack. Was informed that it did not take place for some reason that no one knew. Was ordered back to Vacqueville to attend school. Studied from 10 A.M. to 12 N. Spent the balance of the day answer some letters I received this morning. Returned to my camp in the woods with the mess detail at 5 P.M. Was assigned to a post, in charge of a auto rifle squad. About a mile from camp, just in rear of the artillery. This is my post of alert and am not required to remain awake. The best place I could find to sleep was the bottom of a half finished trench. I no sooner got to sleep when it began to rain. All the protection I had is a blanket. This soon became saturated as did the ground about me. The artillery became active about 2 A.M. and gave up all idea of getting any sleep.

Sunday July 14

This is France's Independance {*sic*} Day. Gen. Pershing has declared this a holiday for all American troops not in the line. We being in reserve, could not benefit by this holiday. Spent the morning cleaning my equipment & auto rifle. It surely needed cleaning after last night's rain. Retired in the P.M. Went to my post at dusk. Just about got comfortably set when it began to rain. It rained spasmaticly {*sic*} all night. At times it poured, but despite the fact that I was lying in mud & water I slept fairly well. I can sleep any place now.

Monday July 15

Attended school at Vacquesville during the day. Attempted to return to my platoon in the woods without a guide. After an hours walk I discovered I had taken the wrong path and had to retrace my steps. After 3 hours walking I finally arrived at our little camp. I should have made the trip in half an hour. As it was I arrived just in time to be too late for supper and had to be satisfied with a slice of bread and a cup of coffee. My post of alert was changed to-night because the Germans were expected to give us a little trouble. Four men & myself had an auto rifle with which to guard the main road on which they might advance. Aside from some of our artillery fire all was quiet during the night.

> On July fifteenth came word that the long expected German blow had fallen on the Marne, bringing something of relief to the troops of Lorraine, and on the sixteenth the French were withdrawn from the sector.

WHISPERS IN THE WIND .89.

Tuesday July 16

Attended school in the morning and completed my course as intelegence *(intelligence–ed.)* observer. No one can now dispute my claim of possessing intelegence {*sic*}. Returned to my platoon at noon. Made absolutely sure that I was following the right path this time. Rested all P.M. Rolled my pack and prepared to leave for somewhere's {*sic*} to-night. No one is certain as to where we are going.

> That night I withdrew the whole garrison of Neuviller, save one outpost in the west end of town, establishing a new platoon headquarters at St. Agathe. We crept out in silent procession over the starlit meadows, picking our way across the wake of the old artillery barrage which showed like a line of trenches in the darkness. It is important that the enemy should not know that the village would be left empty at night.

Left the woods about 10 P.M. as we were relieved by another platoon. Walked in the direction of Vacquesville and we were surprised when we were led to our billets about 45 minutes later. we had expected to move to the front line. Made my bunk and retired. The night is very warm.

Wednesday July 17

Was selected to take charge of 25 men and lead them to the quarry, where they were put to work to make little ones out of big ones. The day is very hot and my sympathy is with the men, if that will do them any good. Brought the men back for mess at noon. They were all tired, hot and drenched with perspiration. I was relieved in the afternoon and another corporal took charge of them. I took advantage of this opportunity to take a bath in a near by stream and try to drown a few cooties. I also washed my under clothes and O.D[49]. Shirt. This left me striped {*sic*} to the waist so I lied in my bunk while my clothes dry in the hot sun. Gee but it's hot. Received a batch of letters. Retired & read them by candle-light.

Thursday July 18

Cleaned my equipment in the A.M. Rested most of the P.M. Rolled my pack and am ready to move into the front line to-night. Started at 9 P.M. arrived at destination about midnight. Waited around until about 2 A.M. while the guard was being posted. Was not selected for guard duty. Snatched a little sleep in an old hut in the woods.

Friday July 19

At daylight I pitched my tent in the woods. I learned that we are holding the front line in the same place where our company was attacked the last time we were in the line. We are better prepared for them now and know they won't be as frisky as they were and get away with it. Slept most of the day. About 6 P.M. a Jerry[50] machine came over and created quite a disturbance. Our guns got after him. Later two of our planes succeeded in driving him away. One artillery battery of ours sent over quite a number of shells without receiving any in return. Lied down after supper so as to be rested when I go on patrol to-night.

Saturday July 20

Went out on patrol shortly after midnight with my lieu-tenant and party of about 15. We made the rounds of all our posts, including a few in no man's land, to see that everything is O.K. As we returned about 3 A.M. our artillery opened up with a barrage which lasted for 75 minutes. The 306th followed it over the top and attacked the Germans. We stood alert until daylight and then lied down for a rest. Three of our planes were out observing the damage done by our artillery this morning. German's guns and machine guns opened fire on them. The shrapnel was bursting over our heads at times & our tin hats seemed mighty usefull {*sic*}. One sergeant & myself went out to post the new guard. Started about 7 P.M. and did not return until 12:30. We wandered around the ruins of Neuviller. All was desolate & quiet. It reminds one of a haunted place. Was glad to get back & get some sleep.

Sunday June 21 (July 21)

Slept all morning. While in the act of shaving, about 2:30 P.M. I heard a few shots fired from the enemy's direction. I quietly grabbed my rifle, belt & bayonet and rushed to my post in my undershirt. All the boys jumped to their feet and all were on the alert in a jiffy. Our captain came around to our various posts and informed us that Co. B. had gone over the top on a daylight raid to try to capture that troublesome machine gun. The sounds of machine gun fire, rifle fire, & exploding bombs lasted about ½ hour. We were then told it was all over & hoped our boys succeeded in their attack.

It having been determined that on July twenty-first the Americans should launch a blow, at 2 P.M. of that day, the First Battalion again holding the line, *(they had relieved the Third Battalion in a rotating fashion–ed.)* Captain Barrett of B Company led out some fifty men through the thick woods. A way had been cut through the very heavy wire in front, but there was no artillery preparation, and the raid was conducted in broad daylight—presupposing a thinly held enemy line and surprise. Whether or not the enemy had obtained advanced information, or merely had accomplished very quickly their preparations after warnings from scouts, it is impossible to determine. The American force had advanced several hundred yards, and, after cutting through some more heavy wire, out of the silence came the clear notes of a German Bugle. Like the clarion blare of trumpets, when the curtain rose on an old-world pageant, that brief tragedy opened. A line of German infantry rose up in a trench in front; enfilading machine guns opened up on either flank, and across the wire auto-rifles fired from the trees in the rear. To the undying credit of Captain Barrett be it said that he ordered and led a charge. His one lieutenant with a third of the men, was sent to cut through the wire to the rear, while the remainder of the force, against hopeless odds tried to clear the front. Poor, brave, beloved Captain Barrett, with his little silk Confederate flag folded in his breast pocket, to fly from the first enemy trench captured—never was the flag of the Lost Cause more gallantly borne, nor to more utter disaster. Of that charging line not one man came back, the captain reeling from a wound and staggering on to death, and of those taken prisoner only one was unwounded. But the others, the lieutenant and sixteen men, came through, and two were unhurt. The score of the first battalion was mounting.

About 5 P.M. my Lieutenant told me to take fourteen men and relieve A Co. further back in the woods and the balance of the platoon would follow. We relieved them about 8 P.M. and after pitching our tents I posted the guard and waited for the rest of the boys. They arrived about midnight and I showed them where to camp. I was then relieved by another corporal and turned in about 1:30 A.M.

Monday July 22

Awakened at 3 A.M. to stand alert. After which I posted the day guards. I tried to snatch a little sleep after breakfast. My slumbers were disturbed about 10:30 A.M. by the bursting of shrapnel & shells overhead. These were directed at three of our scouting planes which were observing the enemy positions. Heard that our boys suffered heavy losses in yesterday's attack. Slept during most of the P.M. Posted guard in the evening. All was quiet until about 12:30 A.M. when I was to be relieved. Just as I was awakening the other relief, Jerry's artillery opened up & let loose. The shells seemed to be falling close so I woke up the Lieutenant & the rest of the boys and all took our posts of alert. By this time our artillery commenced firing. It turned out to be an artillery dual which lasted until 2 A.M. Our boys deserved the decision. They sent over at least two shells to his one. His guns were silenced about 1:15 A.M. When all was quiet once more we all went to sleep suffering no damage.

Tuesday July 23

Awakened at 3:30 A.M. Stood alert after which I went on guard duty again. Relieved at 1 P.M. and slept all afternoon. Rolled my pack in the evening. It rained hard and made the ground slippery & muddy. Our platoon was relieved about 7:30 P.M. and we moved further back in the woods. Our platoon sent out an ambush patrol with instructions to get prisoners if possible. They left about 10:30 P.M. I am corporal of the guard and was relieved at 12:30 A.M. after which I went to sleep.

Wednesday July 24

"Up & at 'em" at 3:00 A.M. Our patrol is just returning, tired & sleepy also disappointed. They went as far as "Jerry's" third line without seeing a soul. Rested most of the day. Was paid this afternoon and am 135 francs richer. Retired to my dog tent after standing alert. My slumbers were disturbed about midnight by heavy machine gun fire from our guns. Lasted about 20 minuets{*sic*} after which silence reigned once more.

Thursday July 25

"Rose & Shone" at 3:30 A.M. Fetched some water in a bucket before mess and had a refreshing wash. My first one in three days. Slept all morning except for about 15 minutes when my sleep was disturbed by shots fired at our scouting planes. While in charge of a detail to get some sand bags I met some A. Co. men who informed me that some of their men had captured three German prisoners in Neuviller.

> One patrol under the Captain of Company A captured three German prisoners at a church in Neuviller after living there, between unsuccessful efforts at surrender, for nearly a day and a night.

This was good news. Our battalion is the first of the National Army to capture any prisoners. They gave some valuable information. They said Cpt. Barrett of B. Co. & 14 men were buried by them.

> Captain Barrett, it was said by prisoners, was buried by the Germans with full military honors.

Rested most of the afternoon. We are sending another ambush patrol out tonight. I am corporal of the guard to-night. Was ordered to take my blanket and sleep near my post of alert. Found a soft spot amongst some dried leaves and slept soundly.

Friday July 26

Slept all morning after standing alert from 3:30 to 4:45 A.M. Did a little light fatigue with the boys about the trenches in the afternoon. Learned that the ship Justicia on which we came over, had been sunk about a week ago. We all mourn her loss. The captain of the ship had made a bost {sic} when he was bringing us over, that he would be taking us back in September. We all feel sorry that he can't make good his promise. Slept near my post of alert. Made my tour of inspection at 12 M. and found everything O.K.

Saturday July 27

Awoke about 2:30 A.M. to find the rain comming {sic} down in torrents. My blanket was soaked through and I soon became drenched to the skin. I had to stay at my post until 5 A.M. in the downpour without any shelter. Spent the balance of the day in my dog tent while the sun & rain played tag. The trenches are a mighty uncomfortable when it rains. The squads of the platoon were rearranged. I am now in charge of the rifle grenade squad known as the "artillery of the infantry". It rained mighty hard while I was at my post of alert and all was pitch dark. It is my duty to stay on my post until morning, but as my tent is only 50 yards away I could not see any justice in the order. I placed a guard on duty and sneaked off to my tent and found things about as bad there.

Sunday July 28

Awakened about 2:30 A.M. to make my tour of inspection. The weather was as bad as before. It was impossible to see your hand before your face. I know I would never be able to find the posts and would probably wander into the woods and become lost so I sneaked back to my tent expecting a call down in the morning. My excuse was that I became lost and returned to my tent after wandering around an hour. I got away with the excuse. Stayed in my tent all day. Rolled my pack in the afternoon after the rain had stopped. Everything was wet and my pack seemed to weigh a ton. Waited about all night expecting to be relieved by another division.

Monday July 29

Our relief, the 37 division Ohio National Guard, arrived at 2:30 A.M.

> On the night of the twenty-ninth, began the relief of the regiment by the 146th Infantry, 37th Division, the latter taking over first the support positions. The Second Battalion took over the front from the First Battalion on the thirtieth.

Without having had any sleep we started our hike to Baccarat if we could make it before dawn. Arrived in Vacqueville at 4:30 A.M. where we were billited {sic} and rested all day. Rolled my pack ready to resume march at 8:30 P.M. Left at time scheduled & arrived at Baccarat at 10:30 P.M. About all the beds were in use so we had to be content with sleeping on the floor. Am very tired & know it won't take long before I fall asleep.

Tuesday July 30

Rested all day. Been scouting through the barracks & found a cot with a spring. Confiscated same immediately and am determined to get a good night's sleep. My sound slumbers were aroused about 11:00 P.M. by the blowing of a strobon[51] horn which is a signal that enemy planes are about & to seek shelter.

> I walked at the head of the column with a sergeant clasping to his breast the huge strombos horn used for alarms of a wave-gas attack, and, having jumped the brook, asked him if he could make it. "Easily sir", he answered, as he fell flat on his chest across it, and "Booooooooom" went the great horn, echoing out across the silent meadows, while, over the wide battalion, startled soldiers snatched on their gas masks and prepared for death. When at last we had choked it off we could only sit where we were and laugh till we were tired.

After 15 minutes of machine & anti-aircraft gun fire, Jerry was driven away and finished my much needed sleep.

Wednesday July 31

Waited about all morning for a bath which we did not receive. We are attached to Co I and had to drill with them in the P.M. Returned late to find no supper had been saved for us. Ate in town and retired early.

Thursday Aug 1

Hiked to Merviller for a bath a distance of three miles. Were told that we should have reported yesterday and that their schedule could not be changed. Hiked back sorely disappointed & just as lousy. Was "on our own" for the balance of the day.

Friday Aug 2

Received that muchly {*sic*} needed bath this morning. Inspection this afternoon also one hour's close order drill. Wandered around town the balance of the day. Am corporal of the guard this evening.

Saturday Aug 3

Free all day to wander about town. Enjoyed some movies at the YMCA and retired early.

Sunday Aug 4

"On my own " to do as I pleased. Rolled my pack at 5 P.M. ready to move by 9 P.M. Left on time amidst a heavy shower. Did not last long but helped just to make things uncomfortable. We hiked for 50 minutes & rested for 10 every hour. It was a hard hike but we stuck it out.

> **It was an exhausting night of endless hills, and on one, almost at its most exhausting stage, when sore feet had become an agony and the burden of heavy packs intolerable, when hope no longer suggested that each hill may be the last, nor that there was any last hill to hope for, sullen and**

cursing men began to throw themselves down by the roadside.

Fell asleep at each halt.

Monday Aug 5

Finally arrived at Saranville[52] at 3:30 A.M. after 6 ½ hours of hiking. Was darn tired and was glad to get in Hotel Barn. Slept until noon. Washed up & bathed my feet. Rested the balance of the day. Listened to a band concert by our regimental band in the evening & retired early.

Tuesday Aug 6

Was surprised when told we would drill to-day. Drilled all morning in close order, extended order, bayonet & musketry drills. Prepared for inspection this P.M. Rained & inspection was cancelled much to our regret. Rain stopped after mess. Listened to band concert & retired early. Informed we would rise early to-morrow & continue our march.

Wednesday Aug 7

Awakened at 6 A.M. and told that I was "out of luck" for breakfast. The men had already eaten & were rolling their packs. I argued with the mess sergeant. He shut me up by giving me a piece of bread & cup of coffee. Rolled my pack hurriedly and started on our hike at 7:30 A.M. Passed through some beautiful farm lands.

We remained in the area until August seventh. Then came a pleasant daylight march through the sunny forest of Charmes to a bivouac among the beeches of its southwestern edge; and on the

eighth the regiment entrained at Charmes for the Marne.

Last night's rain helped to keep the dust down and made marching more pleasant. After hiking 12 K. we stopped in a field for lunch. Continued at 1:30 P.M. Marched 7 K. more and stopped in the woods 4.5 K. from Charmes. Told we would start again early in the morning. So we made ourselves as comfortable as possible & snatched a little sleep.

Thursday Aug 8

Awakened at 1 A.M. Cold & chilly. Warmed up at a nearby campfire. Left at 1:30 A.M. and arrived at Charmes about 2:30 A.M. where we entrained after hiking 45 kilos since we left Baccarat. Crowded as usual in our cattle car pullmans. Train left Charmes at 4:30 A.M. Too crowded to attempt to sleep. Crouched in a corner & watched the passing scenery. Rode south to Épinal then changed our course in a NW direction. Passing Bar Le

Duc & Neuf Chateau{*sic*}[53]. We were side tracked about ½ hour for each meal. Arrived at La Ferte Caucher[54] about midnight and detrained.

The night of the ninth was spent in and about La Ferte Gaucher, at St. Simeon, and Jouy-sur-Marne.

Friday Aug 9

Marched about 3.5 kilos and lied down in a open field outside of a village. Slept all morning. Received permission to visit the village for an hour. The name of this village is so large I did not trouble myself to remember it *(Jouy-sur-Marne–ed.)*. Nothing of interest in same. Attended N.C.O. meeting this evening. Captain told us we would move to-morrow to an active front. Pitched my tent & retired.

Saturday Aug 10

Sent a cable gram home, not knowing when I would be able to write again. Rolled my pack. Moved out at 10:30 A.M. Hiked about 3 miles in a hot sun with our heavy packs. Finally boarded lories.

> At noon of the tenth the troops were loaded on motor busses for the north. It was an interesting though exhausting twelve hour ride through the wake of recent battles—the half ruined villages, the huddled rifle pits, the shell craters, graves and the trampled wheat-fields where the charging feet had passed. Château-Thierry was already filling with civilians, patient old men and women returning to their gutted and windowless homes, amidst the still persistent odor of decay.

Sixteen of us were crowded in each one. Lorries could be seen all along the road as far as the eye can see. We ate our dinner consisting of hard tack & canned hash which we received before we started. About 2:30 P.M. the long train of lories got in motion. We were indignant to find them going back the same direction from which we had hiked. We sat cramped in these trucks for seven hours with nothing to eat but the dust of the roads. Our lories were driven by Chinese from some French colonies. They certainly are reckless drivers. Many times they had the trucks running on one side. I know it is much safer in the front line trenches than to ride on these coolie driven lories. Passed through Chateau Thierry{*sic*} about 6:30 P.M. Were met by some red cross workers who threw some chocolate in our trucks as we passed. This must have been a pretty town, but now it is in complete ruins. From now on we passed through territory from which the Germans were driven back by the France-

American troops. The wheat fields and all the surrounding country are full of big shell holes. Every building in the towns through which we pass is in ruins. We speak to some of our boys as we stop occasionally. They tell us of the things that are happening here. The fighting has been fierce. The Germans are retreating so fast we cannot keep up with them. Women prisoners have been captured chained the machine guns as well as lads of 14 & 15 years. We finally arrived at Fer en Tards[55] at 9:30 P.M.

> **The regiment arrived toward midnight at Fère-en-Tardenois, groping its way on foot through the block of traffic in the ruined town to the wooded hill above, and sleeping broadcast through the bushes where the German dead had not yet all been gathered.**

This was a big German base which was taken by our boys about 10 days ago. We got off and hiked out of the town into the woods. We tramped over fallen trees, shell holes & trenches. The woods are so dense & the night so dark we became all confused and the men from the different companies became messed up. We finally were told to lie down where we were & things would be straightened in the morning.

ILLUSTRATIONS

Map of the 307th Regiment's theater of operation

Sergeant Jack Leonard Horn

The United States of America
honors the memory of

JACK L. HORN

This certificate is awarded by a grateful
nation in recognition of devoted and
selfless consecration to the service
of our country in the Armed Forces
of the United States

Ronald Reagan

Memorial certificate signed by President Reagan

The original three diaries of Jack L. Horn

Cover page of the second volume of Mr. Horn's diary

Sample pages from the original diary

VOLUME III

August 11—May 9, 1918

August 11, Sunday

Awoke about 7 A.M. Walked a few steps to locate the rest of my company. Heard the mess call. Tried to retrace my steps to where I slept to get my mess kit but could not find same. I seemed to be walking in a circle. After half hour's search I found some of my comrades and we finally located the place. Was almost too late for breakfast and I am starved. Looked about me after mess and saw many things that the Germans left behind in their retreat.

The surrounding area confined its relics for the most part to cooking utensils, feather quilts, and steel helmets. The area was nearly paved with

the latter, that being apparently the article which
the German always first discards when hurried.

Steel helmets, caps, clothing. gas masks, ammunition and
hand grenades were a few of them. Many signs printed in
German can be seen all about us. Everything indicates a hasty
retreat by the Germans. In the afternoon I decided to ex-
plore the woods further and look for some souviners{*sic*}. All
the boys were gathering them. Saw some large shells about 4
feet high which is a great loss to Germany. Saw an allied
plane which had crashed to the ground and was in splinters.
The aviator, an American was buried where he had fallen by
the Germans on July 31, 1918. Also located a pure spring
which was a welcome sight. Water is very scarse{*sic*} here.
We must be cautious of the water we drink in the districts
vacated by Germans. They often poison the wells before
they retreat. They resort to various cowardly tricks. We buried one of our boys this morning who while picking up a German helmet was blown to smithers by a mine which had been
placed beneath it. Strings attached to many objects which
when moved would explode mines. Have found throughout
this district.

August 12 Monday

Awakened by the sounds of numerous bugles which
sounded revelle{*sic*}. The entire company took part in sham
battles. We successfully carried an attack on imaginary machine gun nests. Looked over the town of Fere in
Tardenois{*sic*} and took notice of the ruins. Pianos as well as
other furniture could be seen within the ruins. The
airoplanes{*sic*} are pretty active to-day. One German plane
after bringing down our observation balloons was brought
down by our planes.

Toward sundown the hostile aeroplanes would come over, in twos or threes, for an attack on the observation balloons, very often successful, and would turn back from their flaming victim scarcely bothering to rise out of range above the drumming machine-guns; nor did they ever seem to pay the penalty for their bravado.

The artillery is active also.

Tuesday August 13

Drilled this morning and part of this afternoon. Rolled our packs and are ready to move into the reserve to-night. Started at 9 P.M. and hiked until 1:30 A.M. Some parts of the road were resently{*sic*} repaired and covered with loose rock making walking very difficult especially with our heavy packs. We had to fall out at the side of the road and lie flat on the ground at one time. A very light[56] was dropped from an airoplane{*sic*} illuminating the place like the sun. We were not certain if the plane was one of our own or not, but we took no chances. Another time gas alarms were heard close to us and we stopped to put on our masks hurriedly. Finally arrived in the woods near Bruys[57] tired and sleepy.

Wednesday Aug 14

Had breakfast consisting of coffee and hard tack at 8 A.M. Spent the balance of the morning digging a shelter for myself to protect me from bursting shells. Because of the difficulty to obtain water we did not eat dinner until 4:30 P.M. The artillery on both sides is quite active. Many airoplanes{*sic*} are reconnectering{*sic*} about all day. The sky seems to be poiferated{*sic*} with shells that have been shot at them. Retired early. Awakened about midnight when a ration wagon lost its way and came close to my tent knocking it down and giving my comrades and myself quite a fright. We imagined we would be run over. We riped{*sic*} the back of our tent open and dashed out several other men had narrow escapes. After the driver apologized we felt relieved. I suppose a "pardon me" would have mended any broken limbs which might have resulted from the carelessness. A heavy bombardement{*sic*} lasted all night.

Thursday Aug 15

Was told of a stream nearby. Set out to find same immediately after mess. After 15 minutes search found several shell holes of water closely linked to-gether{*sic*} giving it the apperance{*sic*} of a young stream. The water was not exactly clean but it more than answered the purpose. Drilled a few hours. Rested the balance of the day.

Friday Aug 16

Awakened several times during last night by gas alarms.

The swish and shock of falling bombs with extravagant pineapple forms of fire springing from the earth; or from the misty valley bottom, where the heavy artillery was thundering, would come the red flare of explosions, hoarse shoutings and the blowing of claxton gas alarms.

The German guns were active but no great quantity of gas reached our sector. We suffered no casualties. Attended a non-com- meeting after we watched the 2nd {*sic*} manovers{*sic*}. Our battalion repeated the show in the afternoon. At 4 P.M. I went on battalion guard for twenty four-hours.

Saturday Aug 17

Quiet all day except for an air battle fought this afternoon. Two of our aviators collided and both came tumbling down from the sky. They were killed instantly.

> Once, at noon, two American planes were seen circling directly overhead, and a thousand feet above them, three Germans against the blue. A faint splutter of shots was heard, but the distance was far too great for effective fire, and the danger of the Americans did not seem imminent when they were seen suddenly to crash together and the wing of one to shear off at the shoulder. Down it dropped, dropped, dropped, slowly, swiftly, and then with appalling speed, gathering impetus with every fathom, nose first, in one plummeting chute, the sunshine gleaming on its painted sides and the whirr of its motors growing to a deafening roar, sliding like a lost soul through thousands of feet of air, a glistening living thing headed for utter destruction; and it struck, in a pile of crumpled debris, at the edge of wood. The other, reeling from the blow, came down in a staggering spiral, almost under control, fouled in the top of some cottonwoods below the hill, and turned end over on to the ground. Each had carried only a single man, and Lieutenants Smythe and Wallace were buried side by side.

Retired early. Heavy shelling during the night.

Sunday Aug 18

Had some practice in shooting some rifle grenades. They are very powerful & also very dangerous. One of the grenades exploded in one of the cups which are attached to the rifle. It is miraculous that the one who shot it was not killed. No one was hurt however. We were out manuevering{*sic*} over the fields in the afternoon. Running, dashing and falling over hills and dales. Covered with deep shell holes we finally reached our objective after three hours. We returned dirty & tired. Two battalions of our regiment moved out to the front line this evening. Retired.

Monday Aug 19

Heavy continuous bombardment last night. The entire battalion was ordered to help the engineer construct a new system of trenches. The section which we are digging is located on top of a steep hill which overlooks a vast spray of land. We can almost see the German lines. I can see light enemy observation balloons.

> Our platoon, alone, was under observation by balloons. A line of trenches had been laid out on some lower ground, here the thick trees seemed to offer adequate protection from observation, and work upon them was begun by details from the four companies.

Our artillery can be seen scattered about the landscape screened from enemy observation by the many patches of woods. In the afternoon the enemy artillery were trying to locate our artillery. They fired a great number of shells. It was very entertaining to watch them burst throwing the dirt high into the air and to hear them whistling through the air &

hear the great report. Of course the thing that made them more pleasing was that they burst about 2 miles away.

> **Three German planes were seen through the leaves hovering high overhead and soon the shells began ranging in. So accurate was the fire and efficient the observation that, among the first half-dozen shells, one broke on the lip of the trench, wounding four men who lay prone on the bottom.** *(Two miles makes a huge difference in the simultaneous realities of the respective soldier groups. I would imagine that had Sgt. Horn known how effective the shelling really was in relation to his comrades two miles away, the display might have been much less pleasing.—ed.)*

Quit work at 4 P.M. Nothing to do until to-morrow.

Tuesday Aug 20

Heavy bombardement{*sic*} again last night. Hiked to the trenches we were digging yesterday to continue our work. Witnessed a continuation of yesterday's artillery duel. Suffered from a toothache & visited the regimental dentist this afternoon. Wrote some letters and rested the balance of the day.

Wednesday Aug 21

Went through some maneuvers this morning. We were excused this afternoon to clean up. Took a bath in that would-be stream also washed some clothes. Felt a little indesposed{*sic*} & retired early.

Thursday Aug 22

Waited about all day evidently expecting some orders. Received our pay this afternoon, but were interupted{*sic*} by an order to roll our packs immediately & be ready to move in 1/2 hour. Moved out on time. We hiked about 2K in a scorching sun with heavy packs causing the persperation{*sic*} to drip off our brows. We stopped in a thick woods and unrolled our packs. We were barely comfortably settled when another order to roll our packs and be ready to move in 15 minutes, was given. We hiked another kilo into another woods & relieved the 2nd batt. We were assigned to individual shelter dugouts & soon made ourselves comfortable for the night.

(The following paragraph is offered not for its relevance to this book, but for its general interest. Keep in mind that this is 1918. Airplanes are primitive low flying affairs with no lights and are therefore flown almost exclusively during daylight hours.–ed.) Once on a still night of midsummer moonshine, there passed a strange flight of projectiles, like a flock of migrating birds, high, high up in the moonlit silence, coming from one knew not where, and traveling with a drowsy note and on even keel to some remote target far in the inaudible distance.

Friday Aug 23

Spent a restful night except that I was awakened many times by the noise of our big guns. Located a spring & enjoyed a good wash. Spent the balance of the day writing letters & reading some papers & magazines from the U.S. Heavy shelling in our immediate vicinity all day & all night.

Saturday Aug 24

Rained this morning until about 9:30 after which we dug trenches near us. Did the same this P.M. until 4:30. Shells were bursting close to us. Clouds of dirt & smoke would rise high into the air every time one struck. Heavy artillery fire during the night.

Sunday Aug 25

Dug trenches from 7:30 to 10 A.M. Were dismissed for the balance of the day. Rolled our packs this afternoon. Left about 8 P.M.

> The night of the twenty-fifth, the Third Battalion was relieved by the First. The First Battalion had taken over the line that night. Their position had been taken up under an interdiction fire from enemy artillery—a statement which inadequately describes the confusion of tired men stumbling about amidst drenching rain, through the thick darkness and underbrush of unfamiliar slopes, and groping under artillery fire for the uncertain protection of rifle pits. Two were killed and four were wounded at this time.

Crossed the field in battle formation & avoided the roads because they are shelled constantly. The shells from our artillery were whizzing over our heads to cover our advance. The enemy's shells were falling about us & we wondered if we would get to the support safely. Arrived in a very thin woods on top of a hill about 10 P.M. & relieved{*sic*} Co. H.. I looked about & soon found a small dugout into which two of us crowded. We were just getting settled when the enemy opened a barrage. The shells were whizzing close & fast.

The gas alarm sounded & I must have broken all records in putting my mask on. Our artillery returned the fire & it turned out to be a lively duel with us in the centre of it. A half hour later we were allowed to remove our masks. Lied down to sleep but was awakened several times by the gas alarm. The shelling kept up all night long by both sides.

Monday Aug 26

Rained early this morning & we had a hard time to keep the water out of the dugout. Only two meals a day while we are here. We dine at 10 A.M. & 5 P.M. Shells bursting about us all day. You can bet I am lying low in my dugout. Every time one bursts the ground about us trembles. The rain & sun alternate in their appearance. The ground is wet & things are mighty uncomfortable. The boys went out on a digging party to-night, but there was more corporals than was necessary so I was excused. I tried to snatch a little sleep but that was hardly possible, with a Jerry plane buzzing overhead dropping bombs. The artillery continued to be very active.

Tuesday Aug 27 *(The Battle of Château Du Diable follows–ed.)*

Aroused about 7 A.M. & ordered to make up our battle packs. Did not know what was to happen but did as we were told. Our artillery soon opened up with a corking barrage. We were then informed that our 2nd battalion was going "over the top" and we might be needed.

The next day a battalion attack was ordered for the dawn of the twenty-seventh. Major Jay, battalion commander, stated that he did not feel it was possible for him to reconnoitre and prepare properly to make the attack on the morning of

the twenty-seventh as had been suggested. An
additional reason for this request was the fact that
the supporting artillery of the regiment would
not be available to support an operation in our
sector. It was determined, however, that the attack would be made on the twenty-seventh.

We waited about, all ready for action with the shells whizzing overhead for about half an hour.

Meanwhile, that morning a German prisoner just
captured, brought word that a German general
attack along the same sector was prepared for the
morning of the twenty-seventh—which promised
ill for the reception of ours.

We were then permitted to remain on the alert in our
dugouts. The barrage quieted down about 8:30 A.M. and we
snatched a little sleep. While we were eating our morning
meal of bread, butter, & coffee we could see some of the
wounded coming up to the first aid station. We heard from
them, that our lines had been advanced a mile.

Very little intercommunication was possible between the various portions of the line, and this
only by devious routes. Both flanks were very
open and ill-defined, and much of the ground
was debatable.

Shelling continued all day as usual. After evening mess I
was ordered to roll my pack and report to Co. Hdqtrs with 8
men. Met men from other companies of the batt. and learned
we would form a relay liasian{sic}. We were led by a guide
who did not seem certain of the way and consequently did a
good deal more walking than necessary.

Maps of the region were scarce, were all of very small scale, and of a particularly perishable quality of paper all leading to very possible errors in the locating of positions.

It began to rain but we continued and soon became drenched. We walked for about two hours through woods so dark that you could see only a short distance before you.

The absence of any clear knowledge of the enemy's strength or disposition—for little of this could be gathered from the troops relieved—the very vague and non-continuos nature of the line, and the lack of any natural position of strength or shelter, from which an assault might be launched, or to which, in case of unsuccess, withdrawal might be made, rendered the coming attack, delivered as it was to be within the first twenty-four hours of occupation of the line, undoubtedly hazardous. Our Major Jay threw the whole weight of his influence toward obtaining at least a postponement—but did not prevail.

The ground was very slippery and we had great difficulty to avoid falling into the numerous shell holes about.

It was dark when we started, low westward hung the thread of a dying moon, while beneath it grew the dull roar of our attack. Shells were passing overhead while through dense swamp the leading platoons moved forward in column, and at the edge of the open meadow deployed in line.

We finally met a lieutenant at a post who left men at that

post and they followed him. He stopped at each post on the way & left men at each of them to relieve the men who were there. It took at least an hour to post the relief. Of course it was my luck to be on the last post.

(ed. Note—It truly was his luck to be at the most distant outpost because . . .) They did not know the odds against them—it was not known until after the war—they only knew that they were struck by such a blast of fire as made life impossible. Those who were ordered to attempt the open meadow were swept away, while the rest, gaining only a few rods through the neck of the woods, clung there under a steady hail of bullets. At the end there was nothing left there but the German machine guns. The entire meadow platoon was gone, not a man of it came back. Captain Adams and Lieutenant Scudder who had started out in search of it, fell side by side, each shot through the neck as they lifted their heads above an embankment.
That finished it, for no further effort was possible for the troops at hand.

And when we reached it I was so exhausted I was ready to drop. We had walked or ran for about three hours without a rest & carrying full packs. Shells were bursting about us & were expecting to be hit any moment. I was left at this last post, which is batt. Hdqrts of the batt. in the line, in charge of seven men who would act as runners. Was shown the various routes which they would traverse, by the corporal who I am relieving. *(Editor's note—Runners were used extensively in the Great War as a method of communication. Poor communication played a large part in making this war so costly in lives. It was a large-scale war fought with small-scale communication, a huge, deadly machine capable of mass destruction with no one at the controls. Wireless communication was in its infancy and not used in this war. Telephone and telegraph communication were used but wire had to be laid from the battalion headquarters to the field regimental command posts. Then from the field command posts to the front lines. Additionally, wire to the artillery stations was essential. Within minutes of shelling by the enemy these wires would be broken just when they were needed most. The only ways left to convey messages were by carrier pigeon, which was ridiculously unreliable, or the human runner. These men were quite physically fit and courageous. They would take a message from the line or an order from command and run with it through falling artillery shells, sniper fire and machine gun fire to the appropriate recipient. Another runner (or the same one) would then run the reply either up to battalion headquarters or back to the front line. The running method was set up much like the old pony express, with a runner reaching a station where he would hand off the message to a "fresh" runner who would then proceed to the next station and so forth. As time was of the essence, runners were killed wholesale as they were not able to take the time to pay much attention to the dangers around them. When a runner was killed or severely incapacitated the message, be it an order or request, would be lost or even more greatly delayed. Even when the message made its way to the intended recipient, the elapsed time could be several hours. There was no way, therefore, to quickly alert the artillery that their range was too short and that they were shelling their own men. Requests by desperate trench commanders for immediate reinforcement would come too late, if at all. Additionally, if the enemy intercepted the runner, sensitive information could then be used to inflict more casualties. An excellent portrayal of the dangers and inefficiency of the World War One runner system may be seen in the 1981 Australian film Gallipoli.) Machine gun shells & bullets were whizzing about us as we double timed to our destinations. Occasionally{sic}, a very light would shoot up illuminating the place. We had to remain motionless until it died out. After another hour of recountering{sic} we returned to my post situated in a cave which is absolutely shell proof.*

Battalion Headquarters' cave was a vast affair of flickering candles and dim recesses, paved with equipment and sleeping soldiers, over which one entering picked his tortuous way.

The place was overcrowded and I was fortunate to find a place where I could squeeze in and snatch a little sleep.

Long after August twenty-seventh a few of the dead were found among the fallen poplars at the base of Château hill, and some near the far edge of the woods, but for the most part the battleground was left in the hands of an enemy who glean it well.

The price was heavy—of officers, three wounded and four missing, of whom only one, Captain Adams, ever returned alive after the armistice, and of the men, sixteen killed, eighty-four wounded and forty missing, presumed dead—one hundred and forty men.

The attack had failed, and yet, with the clearer knowledge we now have of that against which the attack was launched, it may be that its bloody failure should be reckoned a success of sorts. For the devotion of the men to their appointed task held immobile before them a force perhaps six or eight times their number that was intended to attack; and the blow they struck against it, however impotent to achieve their purpose, served at least to prevent what might have been a disaster to the battalion and the line. There can be no estimate of the enemy loss, though to have so

completely paralyzed their initiative, it must have
been heavy.
The night of August twenty-seventh saw the sector practically unchanged.

*(This was a tragic scenario throughout World War One on both
the western and eastern fronts. Hundreds, often thousands of men
would fight the enemy for days or weeks in a given section of the
line. Hundreds often thousands would die or end up horribly
wounded over these days or weeks only to find themselves in relatively the same place as when they started. Even more senseless would
be the slaughter of thousands of men in order to win ground which
would then be given up voluntarily a few weeks or months later
because it was no longer of strategic significance.–ed.)*

Wednesday Aug 28

We brought some hard tack and canned goods with us
and that must last us until we are relieved. No food can be
bought up here.

**Losses from artillery and machine-gun fire were
very constant, and the life—lying all day in the
shallow rifle pits, eating sparingly of such food as
they had brought with them, and drinking the
water of the polluted river—was wearing in the
extreme.**

I was placed in charge of an additional relay from here to
the front line trenches. I posted my men at the various stations. We had to keep low to avoid observation and snipers.
Shells were whizzing .overhead but we are getting
accostomed{*sic*} to them now and know just when to duck. It
took me three hours to make the rounds and often climbing
up hill and sliding down dole, cutting through woods, running

through open fields in plain view of the enemy, returned tired & covered with mud. Near the lines the trails are strewn with equiptment{*sic*} of every description, that had been discarded by the troops. I took charge of all messages coming and going and had them relayed to their proper destinations with the aid of my runners. At night the batt. in the line was relieved by the 3rd.

> On the night of August twenty-eighth the Third Battalion relieved the Second Battalion on the front line. The Third Battalion had by now spent ten days on the Red Line *(the reserve line behind the front line–ed.)*—the days spent largely in trench digging and many of the nights in carrying ammunition to the forward battalion of the brigade. It was not a period of much physical exhaustion, but the strength of the men was sapped with dysentery, and the shell-fire on the two rear companies had been constant. Every officer but one was already a casualty, and that remaining lieutenant was killed by a direct hit of a shell on their first day in the forward position.

I was then ordered to post reliefs{*sic*} on the route to the front line. It took me four hours to do this and went through the same experiences as before. Returned at 1:30 A.M. and was all in.

Thursday Aug 29

Was awakened several times by gas alarms and had to keep our masks on for about 1/2 hour at a time. Aroused about 5 A.M. by heavy shelling about the cave. Shells were striking on top and very close to us. They could not damage the cave as it was made of heavy rocks, but the concusion{*sic*} could be felt every time one struck. It lasted about 1/2 hour. One man being killed & two wounded. Was busy with messages all day which had to be delivered through heavy shell fire at times. Our rations are almost exhausted and no other food in sight. Was told we would be relieved to-night. Relief arrived about 10 P.M. and showed the new corporal his duties. After 1/2 hours search I was unable to find the men of one of the posts. I had to wait until day light to finish posting the men. The cave is overcrowded and I cannot find a place to sleep. Remained awake almost all night.

Friday Aug 30

At daylight I finished posting my relief and was ready to return to my company by 7 A.M. Guided my way back going from post to post. Reported back to the company about 9 A.M. And was given some coffee and believe me it tasted good. Rested the balance of the day. Aroused several times during the night by gas alarms. Heavy shelling as usual.

Saturday Aug 31

Rained this morning. Shelling let up a bit. Am informed we move up to the lines to-night. Rolled my battle pack this afternoon and prepared to move to-night. We received additional ammo and started for the front lines at 8 P.M.

That night the Third Battalion was relieved by the First. The First Battalion had taken over the Red Line on the night of the twenty-fifth. This position had been taken up under an interdiction fire from enemy artillery—a statement which inadequately describes the confusion of tired men stumbling about amidst drenching rain, through the thick darkness and underbrush of unfamiliar slopes, and groping under artillery fire for the

**uncertain protection of rifle-pits. Two were killed
and four wounded at this time.**

I acted as guide for my platoon. We were very fortunate
by being favored with a dark night and drew no fire from the
enemy. We arrived at our sector, which is near the cave that I
had been at my last trip up here, at about 9:30 P.M. Were
assigned to individual dugouts & crawled in. There was comparatively little firing during the night but I did not sleep
much. The cooties & mosquitos{*sic*} keeping me awake.

Sunday Sept 1

As soon as it became light enough I dug my hole a little
deeper to make things more comfortable. A few shells fell in
my immediate vicinity causing me to duck several times. The
man's mess kit in the next dugout was smashed by a piece of
shrapnel but no one was injured. Rained most of the day
making things very disagreeable. It has been fairly quiet to-
day but the artillery would open up occassionally{*sic*} as a
gentle reminder that the war is still on. Slept soundly until
11:30 P.M. when I was aroused by the sound of our guns.

**An attack was launched early on the night of Sep-
tember first. The afternoon and evening had been
unusually quiet, until at about 10 P.M., the enemy opened up with 77 mm's and the fire quickly
increased to a heavy barrage. This lasted some
twenty minutes, mixed with machine gun fire.
An American counter-barrage was laid down in
front of the position for about fifteen minutes;
then the enemy attacked with light and heavy
machine-guns, rifle- and hand-grenades.**

We were putting over a barrage of artillery & machine gun fire. An order soon came to get on the alert & prepare for action. About an hour later all was quiet & we resumed our sleep. The night was terribly cold & I was unable to sleep anymore. Our heavy art. kept sending them over during the night.

Monday Sept 2

We remained in our dugouts all morning to avoid being observed by the numerous planes flying overhead. Expect to be relieved to-night. Ordered to report to the Capt. about 11:30 A.M. Told to take 3 guides & myself & report back in support to ascertain who was to relieve us. Also to reconocter{*sic*} their grounds and learn how to place our men when we take over their positions. The day is clear & we must cross an open field for about 2 miles. We were half way over when we were observed. Their artillery soon shelled us & we were compelled to "hit the dirt" about 15 times. Some of the shells came very close causing shrapnel to fall around us. It still remains a mystery to me how we all escaped un-hurt. Arrived at our destination about 2 o'clock. We received something to eat & felt better. After a short rest I explored the vicinity to find the shortest roads to get here. This occu-pied my time until 7:30 P.M. Just before the time to start back (8:30 P.M.) the enemy began shelling our route heavily and we were compelled to wait until 10:30 P.M. The night is very dark and our progress very slow. We had to stop several times to look for parts of the company I was guiding back, which had broken away from the main body. Numerous very lights were flashed. We undoubtedly observed and soon shelled. We changed our course several times to avoid his range. As we arrived at our destination we were observed again and several gas shells were dropped amongst us. We put our masks on in double time. I was relieved here by another guide & reported to my C. O. & informed him that the plans had been altered a bit. He was unaware of the fact & I had to find the C.O. of our relieving Co. to explain. His P.C.[58] is about 1/2 mile away. While guiding him back we were shelled again and had to take it on the run. Was ordered to remain with my Capt. until further orders. All but my platoon had been relieved of my company. They were sent further up the line. It is now 2 A.M. and I am bookoo{*sic*} fatigue.

Tuesday Sept 3

Called by the Capt. at 7 A.M. & ordered to find my platoon. By means of guards I finally located them after 3 hours search. I delivered my message & returned. It is now about noon. Ate some hard tack & salmon. Tried to sleep a little as I had very little rest last night. Was called again at about 4 P.M. to deliver another message to our platoon at the front. They are about 1 1/2 from Batt Hdqrts. The trip is a rough one to make. Returned at 7:30 P.M. tired thirsty and hungry but could satisfy none of these wants. Told to be ready to join my platoon and leave with the capt at 8:30 P.M. Was not called until 10:30 however & told that the plans had been changed. We will leave at 3 A.M.

Wednesday Sept 4

Called at 3 A.M. Told our platoon would go over the top with A Co. at dawn.

At dawn of September forth, after a brief artillery preparation, under command of Captain Blagden, Companies A and C struck along the railroad tracks south of Château. There was no opposition; the woods where we had suffered so fearfully were empty save for the unburied Ger-

man dead, and a few of the enemy outposts whose
only thought was of escape.

I would remain with the capt. It was still dark when we
made our trip up the line. Upon our arrival I was ordered to
find a Lt from the 308th to whom we would be attached. He
had moved his position and I could not locate him. Returned
just as our barrage commenced. Our platoon formed a Co & I
was sent out to locate the Lt. having a little more information. Finally located him with his Co in an advanced position.
Was shelled as I returned. A piece of shrapnel fell in front of
me & missed me by 2 in. The captain informed the Lt. leaving me at a post to direct anyone who might look for him.
Word soon came back that our boys had advanced and taken
that long disputed hill.

**The companies crossed a highroad under a slight
enfilading fire, and, still unopposed climbed the
hill of the Château where they dug in below a
crest.**

I was ordered to return to Batt Hdqrtrs & obtain a detail
to bring food to our boys in their new positions.

**One shell, of large caliber, wiped out almost the
entire battalion headquarters personnel, together
with two machine-gun officers. Captain Blagden
practically alone remaining unhurt. Fourteen
were killed and ten wounded by this single explosion, and four of the casualties were officers.**

I had no trouble to get 10 men to carry the rations. It was
a risky job to do in the daytime, especially with the skies
infested with airoplanes{*sic*}. I was compelled to remain in
concealment an hour for that reason. Succeeded in reaching

them five hours later and was wellcomed{*sic*} with open arms. Returned to my post & rested most of the P.M. My company is moving forward & I am ordered to join them. Met them at Batt. Hdqrtrs & continued with them through Fisme[59] & Fismette. We were shelled heavily while passing through these towns & had many narrow escapes. All the buildings are in ruins.

> The troops were massed in the town, whose streets were blocked with tumbled debris and wire, and where every courtyard held its unburied dead.

Hardly a wall remians{*sic*} intact. We continued after the Germans who are in a hasty retreat. We stopped for the night on top of a high hill. The 2nd Batt pushing ahead of us.

> The Second Battalion in the meantime, after six days in the rear, advanced into Fismes reaching it about dusk and taking up a temporary position in the ruined cellars of that most desolate town.

Thursday Sept 5

Aroused at dawn to stand alert. The planes were active early. Our position was observed by the enemy and we moved to avoid shelling. Took up a better position a short distance away and dug in.

> At 7 A.M. of September 5th, with a new battalion headquarters organized, the advance was resumed.

After two hours work we were ordered to cease digging & prepare to move forward. Our artillery can be seen moving into position for action. The enemy is shelling near us occasionally{*sic*}. About 3 P.M. we moved forward again slowly & cautiously. Reached a woods on a hill about 700 yards further & dug in. By 9 P.M. I was ready for a good snooze. At 10:30 P.M. a heavy bombardement{*sic*} position commenced. The shells were bursting amongst us.

> As the leading squad-columns reached the high grounds, they were met by machine-gun fire from either flank, and, deploying, attempted to advance in squad rushes. But the fire, increasing in intensity, was mixed now with that of heavy machine-guns and finally with an artillery barrage upon the squirmish line. Every move brought a new burst of artillery fire, for the whole position was under direct observation.

I imagined we would not escape without casualties this time but luck is still with us. About midnight we were ordered to move. Sterot[60] coffee was brought up in the meantime & we were darn glad to get it. This is my first meal since I am in the front line aside of a little iron rations. We slowly advanced another kilo. Reached an important road about 4 A.M. and were assigned to little holes on the side thereof.

Friday September 6
Heavy shelling this morning. Shrapnel flying all around us.

> September sixth and seventh passed without notable event beyond a slow but steady drain of casualties from artillery and machine-gun fire, and a constant drenching gas where the men lay stretched across the swamp-land.

A small piece striking the edge of my dugout & dropping in. No one is hurt. The angles must be with this co. to escape injury throught{*sic*} all the fire we have encountered so far. The shelling continues & we are forced to lay low in our dugouts. The Boche took advantage of this opportunity and crept up on us. He attacked one of our platoons and caught most of them by surprise. Some of our men fell back to my platoon & gave the alarm. We charged and reinforced them. The Boche took to their heels leaving many being on the field behind them. We lost no ground but suffered our first casualties. Heavy shelling continued all day. A shell struck two dugouts from mine buring{*sic*} the occupant. We hurriedly dug him out and found him badly shaken up. The Boche sent over a barrage at dusk and we expected him over again. We stood alert prepared to meet him but he did not come. We changed our position to a line of trenches in the open field. Hardly had we arrived there, when we were shelled heavily again with gas and high explosions. One shell struck the trench above me almost buring{*sic*} me with dirt. When the shelling quited{*sic*} down a bit we moved into the woods we occupied last night. I found a vacant dugout and crept in. Our position has been discovered again and the "footballs" come flying fast & furious.

After dark on the sixth, for nearly an hour an enemy bombing-squadron turned the still night into a chaos of noise and flying debris about their heads.

This continued all night causing us to lie as flat as a pan cake & keep on the alert for gas. The shells were surely comming{*sic*} close and I expected the one with my name on it to reach me at any moment. Was delighted when daylight came & the shelling ceased.

Saturday Sept 7

The Boche thought we had changed our position during the night and his planes are very active anxious to get a line on our whereabouts. But we are exercising supreme precaution and keep under cover. Comparatively few shells struck near us to-day. Water is difficult to obtain and is becomming{*sic*} as scarce as food.

> There was a constant difficulty of ration supply, both in bringing up the transport at night over the shell-swept road, and in distributing to the outlying platoons. There could be little or no attempt at providing cooked food. A ration-dump had been established and then moved without warning of the change to the forward troops. After a night of fruitless waiting at the first location, they got word of the true state of affairs and hurried to the new site just in time to see the entire ration-dump obliterated by the direct hit of an artillery shell.

Iron rations are issued when possible with our midnight meal. A can of bully beef & a box of hard tack must last us all day. Joined my platoon this evening. The Boche welcomed my presence with a rally of shells. Some striking too close to be comfortable. To our discomfort it rained in torrents. The thunder lightning & bursting shells gave me the impression that the end of the world was at hand. After our midnight meal we changed our position again. I am drenched to the skin but that did not prevent me from snatching a little sleep in my mudhole.

Sunday Sept 8

Fairly quiet to-day. Remained in my dugout most of the time. It rained in torrents and I am drenched again. I am cold, hungry, tired & wet. We must be superhuman to withstand sickness under these conditions. Ordered to be ready to "go over" at 7 P.M.

On the evening of September eighth, an order was received calling for an attack. At 6:45 P.M. all companies started forward. A passing shower blew in from the east, and as the troops deployed along the open ground they saw through a veil of glistening rain a rainbow arch—but there was little victory in that fair omen, and much of death.

The troops had no sooner come out upon the meadows than they were met by a hurricane of shells and machine-gun fire. They staggered a short distance forward upon their hopeless way toward the wire lining the front, and then reeled back to the shelter of the woods whence they had come. The troops reformed and passed through the withering machine-gun fire to the edge of a ravine. The losses were bravely taken, but there was never a chance of success and at dusk the men had been drawn back through the smoke from their precarious foothold to their original positions. About 8 P.M. a message was received stating that the supporting artillery for the attack would not open fire until about 7:30 P.M.; *(a prime example of the terribly poor communication between, in this instance, the artillery and the troops and the costly result of this deficiency.—ed.)* and whether or not it did then open fire no one had noticed. No further attack was attempted that night. Before dawn a relief was effected, and the battalion withdrew with an effective strength of 247 men, *or 25 percent of their original number (emphasis mine–ed.).*

It rained in torrents but the attack went on just the same. Just before reaching our objective were ordered to lie down & wait for orders. Some were selected for patroling{*sic*} but I was one of those left behind. It soon became dark & we were seen through the aid of very lights. The shells came a little too fast for us & we returned to co. Hdqts. just as they were moving up to a new position. Had to dig in & lied down about 12 M. in the cold damp hole. I am one mass of mud.

Monday Sept 9

Was improving my hole when the order to prepare to advance came. we were to "go over" at 9 A.M.

This order, whose execution it was, in the first instance, contemplated should take place under the cover of darkness, was actually carried out between 8 and 9 A.M., and the slopes, though appearing on the map to afford probable cover, actually afforded none.

but our artillery's range fell short and hemmed us in. We were also harrased{*sic*} by snipers & machine gun fire. We finally advanced about noon and took our objective which is a ravine infested with snipers & machine guns. We must be very cautious—a close pal of mine was hit when a shell burst near him. I was about 3 feet from him when the accident occured{*sic*}. We suffered quite a number of casualties to-day.

The platoon, looking in vain for its promised shelter, moved down the slope in squad rushes; and at once a battery of field artillery opened upon them with direct fire. Men may speak lightly in retrospect of their dislike for "whizz-bangs," but the point-blank fire of field-guns at a target pilloried in the open is an ordeal to wrench men's souls—the swift rush of sound, the instantaneous crash of the explosion, and then the scream of some disemboweled comrade—again and again, and nowhere on earth to turn for help. The platoon was withdrawn with losses.

Remained under cover until dark & then dug in.

Tuesday Sept 10

Raining very heavily. Ordered to act as guide for a company which will support us. Tramped through mud & water to my knees. Beginning to get weak from this tremendous strain. Returned to my dugout 2 hours later with water dripping off me and covered with mud. Too wet to move. Ordered to advance another half mile after tramping through more mud & woods we reached our objective but found it to be a poor position to hold so we dropped back again. It cleared up late in the afternoon & I worked on my dugout. Established our line of outposts to-night & am in charge of post # 1. One of the men on duty mistook some of my men for the enemy and we had a lively shooting party but no one was hurt.

Wednesday Sept 11

Remained on outpost all day. Very little action during the day. Am occupying a dugout built & previously occupied by

Germans. By the appearance and construction I imagine they had intentions to remain here for quite a while. It is like living in a palace compared with those hurriedly dug holes in the ground. At dusk another man & myself crawled down the valley to try to recover the body of one of our sergeants. We were close to him when the Germans started a dandy barrage. We rushed back to our post and prepared to meet the Hun who we expected to follow the barrage over. All quieted down after an hour however. We expected to be relieved at 8 P.M. but waited until midnight. Our company assembled at Batt Hdqts and we had visions of a bath with clean clothes, some hot meals and a few good nights sleep. We were a disappointed bunch when we were asigned{*sic*} to support trenches which were wet & ankle deep with mud from all the rain we have been getting. The night is terribly cold & we wonder if we can stick it out until morning. There are rumors to the effect that our division will be relieved to-morrow night and we are living in fond hopes and maybe that dream of the baths etc. may yet be realized.

Thursday Sept 12

Remained in the trenches all morning. Received some bread & ground coffee. Made a cup of coffee over a small alcohol flame which took away my chills. It rained spasimatically{*sic*}. Were told we might remain here a few days longer and to dig better shelter. It rained in torrents as we dug and we were soon drenched to the skin. The holes fill with water as quickly as we dig. Managed to make a good dugout after a few hours work and will be more comfortable after I dry up a bit. Little activity to-day.

Friday Sept 13

Remained in my dugout all day. Received our usual ration of rain & shells. Heard we might make another advance to-morrow. Ordered to be ready for same. Sad news after expecting relief so long.

Sat. Sept 14

Barrage started at daybreak. Both artilleries were active & the shells soon were hitting close to us. Ordered to remain in our dugouts ready to move at a moments notice. At about 7:30 A.M. some German prisoners were brought in & we heard that Glanz[61] had been taken.

The French never gained a mastery of Glennes, assuming if indeed they had ever entered it.

A shell struck close to my dugout wounding a sergeant and gassing a number of men. I was fortunate to get my mask on in time and just got a little gas *(editor's note—According to Mr. Horn's son Paul, this "little gas" exposure may have resulted in Mr. Horn suffering from tuberculosis soon after returning from the War for which he spent two years stay in a sanitarium in Upstate New York)*. I helped bring the wounded man to the first aid station when I returned I could see the great damage that had been done. Two boys lied dead & many wounded or gassed. Only 8 remained of our platoon. We assembled all the men of the co. (22 in all) and moved forward in support of the French.

For dawn of September fourteenth another attack was ordered. This opened at 5:15 for half an hour, mixed with an intense indirect fire of machine-guns from the French. The enemy counter-

barrage came down at 5:30, lasting, with drum-fire of 88, 105 and 150 mm shells, almost continuously till eleven. The valley of battle offered a spectacle of unforgettable grandeur. In the earlier darkness some wooden buildings, afire at its mouth, lit a false dawn in the east. Then in the growing light one saw its level meadows cloaked in the mists of morning, and its steep sides shrouded in smoke; they mingled and merged into one vast cauldron of vapor, stabbed through and through with flashes of fire, blotting out the farmsteads beyond, and always through the crash and shock of explosions wove the swift hammer-song of countless machine-guns.

Shells were falling all about us but we continued onward. We lost about 6 more men. We advanced 500 yds & dug in.

The enemy resistance was in no way weakened, but after heavy losses our men dug in along the wire before the line. Here they held during the afternoon and the fighting had seemed over for the day.

Our position is a poor one and we are under heavy shell fire. About 2 hours later we were ordered forward again. A machine gun is our objective.

At 4:55 we received word that a barrage would be laid down along the wire at 5 o'clock. There was no time to protest; there was no time to organize a withdrawal; there was no means of guessing that the barrage would consist of some seven or eight shells which would better have been faced where the companies then were. They streamed back across the meadows, and reorganized under cover for a fresh attack. But this could not be immediately accomplished. The attack, when delivered at dusk, was the most costly yet launched over that trampled, blood-soaked ground. They cut a way through the wire, wiped out the crews of four machine-guns, and established themselves in a German trench.

We formed a skirmish line over an open field & lied down while the first line advanced. We lied there for 2 hours without any orders. Machine gun bullets were whizzing close & digging in the ground around me.

Five officers had fallen in the two attacks—Lieutenant Felter with a bullet through the forehead as he emptied his gun at the muzzle of a machine-gun in action—only one officer was left on the front line.

The alarm that the Boche was counter attacking arrived. We are withdrawn from the field & placed as sentries. It proved to be a false alarm. After dark we took up our position for the night. Heavy shelling continues.

Sunday Sept 15
About 3 A.M. we were ordered to move. It is rumored again that we will be relieved. Placed in dugouts for the night back in support. Helped bring a gassed man to the first aid station and returned to find that my co. had moved because the area has been badly gassed. Stationed at the ration dump. A detail from my company came for rations & I returned with them. Rested all day. Little action in the vicinity. Was told we would be relieved to-night.

Monday Sept 16

It really & finally happened. A division of Italian troops arrived & relieved us at 3 A.M.

> The Italians, who were now waiting to take over the sector, insisted upon a trench, no matter where situated, for them to occupy. The captain, sweeping together whatever troops he could find, filed through the gaps in the wire, reoccupied the trench beyond with a shower of hand-grenades, and turning it over to the Italians, left them to work out their own salvation.
> The relief of the front was decidedly complicated, but nothing noticeable occurred during the day beyond a growing irritation with the Italians. The Italians would demand an explanation of things that no one knew about in a language which no one understood; and meantime there were being sent hither and thither messengers who seldom found the proper recipient of their message, more seldom returned with a reply, and almost never solved the difficulty referred to.

The 16 men that remain of our co. formed the battalion and we are off for a long 10 mile hike. We worked fast and rested very little so that we could get to our destination before daylight & avoid observation . Arrived in a patch of woods about 7 A.M. and joined our kitchen & crew. We, that returned, were an awful looking bunch. Our clothes are torn & tattered. Our face, hands or teeth haven't been washed in these last sixteen days. I have a full grown beard and look like Rip Van Winkle. My muste{*sic*} has such a growth that I have decided to leave it on as a souvenir of the trenches. At my first opportunity I hunted for water. A good wash & shave is treat. Rested the balance of the day. Men who had strayed away from the co. came staggering in bringing our total up to 77 men.

Tuesday Sept 17

Rested all day. Prepared to leave on a long journey tonight. Borded{*sic*} lories at a near by road at 8:30 P.M.

> After dark, having received permission to draw out at their discretion, left the Italians to arrange, after their own manner, their difficulties with themselves and the enemy. The regiment was assembled, during the sixteenth and the seventeenth, some marching, others carried in lorries, half famished and wholly exhausted, in the quiet woods.
> The regiment was being transported to the Argonne. The name meant nothing then, only a vast stretch of forest where nothing occurred, and the regiment little dreamed that its immediate task was to alter that meaning forever.

We were crowded 22 men in a truck and spent a very uncomfortable night. Sleep is impossible.

> The journey by motor trucks was unqualifiedly awful. They were desperately crowded and quite innocent of springs, so that he who found room to sit felt as though perched upon a cocktail shaker; and it lasted for sixteen hours.

Wednesday Sept 18

Arrived at Camp Chatalier[62] in the Argonne[63] Region at about 1 P.M.

> On the afternoon of the eighteenth the troops were unloaded at Le Chatelier and Givrey, remaining there in wooden barracks until evening of the nineteenth.

Delighted at the opportunity to get off those lorries & stretch our weary limbs. Assigned to barns. Spent the balance of the day cleaning up and looking for cooties.

Thursday Sept 19

Checked up on eqipment{*sic*} this morning. Walked to the village and sent a cablegram home. Took a bath in a pond in a downpoor{*sic*} of rain. Ordered to be ready to move at 9 P.M.

> On the nineteenth came word that the regiment would move at night, and all baggage, kitchens, and rations, should be dragged to the road.

Ready to start when told to make our selves comfortable for the night.

> At nine P.M. came word that the regiment would not move, and all baggage etc. was to be returned to the billets.

Friday Sept 20

Awakened about midnight and ordered to get ready again.

> At eleven-ten P.M. came word to move at eleven-thirty.

Started to move when we were halted and told to open our packs and make battle packs. Started again at 1 A.M. Hiked until 10 A.M. arriving at Florentt[64] after covering 32 kilos. Some hike. We are dead tired & lied down imediately{*sic*} after being assigned to dark old shacks.

> After some turmoil, and in a misanthropic frame of mind, not improved by the rain, the Regiment started upon its longest march of thirty-four kilometers. Toward dawn, when the lameness or laziness of the few was giving place to the serious exhaustion of the many, at about nine A.M., the battalions, in admittedly ragged formation, drew into Florent.

Ordered to be ready by 5:30 P.M. to move into the lines.

> Here they had just succeeded in billeting themselves and eating all the eggs in town, when orders came for the battalion and company commanders to proceed at once to the Line of Resistance held by the French four kilometers to the north. The two battalions were to follow and effect the relief of the line that night.

We are now on the Verdun Front. Pulled out at dusk. Hiked through dence{*sic*} woods (Argonne Forest) for about 4 kilos. Arrived at Barracks in the woods. Picked out a good cot and made myself comfortable for the night.

Saturday Sept 21

Supprisingly{*sic*} quiet except for a few planes. Rested all day.

> September 21ˢᵗ to the 23ʳᵈ was of a calm which, it
> became increasingly evident, presaged a storm.

Sunday Sept 22

Ordered to report to Batt Hdqtrs at 9 A.M. Then sent to 3rd Batt to act as liaison between them. Returned on an errand. Too sick to go back & was relieved. After a short rest I felt better. Rained all day.

Monday Sept 23

Awakened at 4 A.M. & told we would move. Hiked about 3 kilos into the woods & pitched tents on the wet ground. Moved back another kilo this P.M. and assigned to bunks in barracks.

Editor's Note- During the next ten days the Second and Third Battalions were on the front line while the First Battalion was behind the line in reserve. What follows is an attempt to inform the reader of what was going on at the front each day that Sgt. Horn was held in reserve

Tuesday Sept 24

> On September 24, the company commanders were
> directed to reconnoiter the front. As seen through
> the slot-like aperture of an observation post over-
> looking a sector of the front line, it seemed quite
> unalluring, and on closer inspection was even
> worse. It was a bleak, cruel country of white clay

and rock and blasted skeletons of trees, gashed into innumerable trenches, and seared with rusted acres of wire, rising steeply into claw-like ridges and descending into haunted ravines, white as leprosy in the midst of that green forest, a country that had died long ago and in pain.

That day the commanders of the units down to and including companies were assembled by the divisional commander and informed that they were about to take part in the greatest offensive yet launched, which would extend from the North Sea to Switzerland, and, it was hoped, would finish the war. Of course it was so hoped, but, by most of the regiment, without exuberant optimism.

Felt indesposed{*sic*}. Suffering from a bad attack of indigestion. Remained in bed all day.

Wednesday Sept 25

On September twenty-fifth the artillery began to arrive. All night long it arrived, crushing and clanking through the underbrush, and in the morning the woods were filled with it, concealed under screens of new-cut leaves. Two hundred guns were massed in the area. In spite of precautions the enemy guessed at attack, though, as was later learned, not on the scale as was being prepared. During the 25th their artillery reached a volume such as the forest had not heard in two years of its peaceful warfare.

Remained in bed all morning. Received some clean clothes & they certainly are welcome. Ordered to report to Batt Hdqtrs then to Div Hdqtrs with 4 men and act as liaison between these points.

> It was hoped that visual liaison would be established by daylight; but it never was. In the many branching trenches squads and platoons became separated in the darkness, or met head-on in the narrow trenches where no passing was possible.

Thursday Sept 26

A drive is to start on this front to-day. Heavy barrage early this morning.

> The artillery, after holding for three and a half hours of drum-fire on the enemy lines, was to advance one hundred yards in five minutes thereafter, and the infantry were to keep within five hundred yards of their rolling barrage—instructions which recurred somewhat hopelessly to the leaders of units during the ant-like wanderings of the morrow.

(The rolling barrage was a technique widely used by both sides during World War One. It was an attempt to compensate for the previously discussed inability of the infantry to communicate in real-time with their artillery. In principle, it consisted of laying down a barrage of artillery shells ahead of the advancing troops. The range of the artillery guns would gradually be increased in yards per minute increments based upon an estimate of the pace at which the troops would be able to move forward The artillery commander and the infantry commander would agree on the calculations prior to the attack. Ideally the barrage would advance at a

pace that would match, but stay ahead of the advance of the troops. In this way the soldiers would, theoretically, have an advancing wall of destruction clearing the path ahead of them. If all went as planned, they would then reach the newly shelled area within a few minutes easily overcoming the dazed enemy soldiers. As can be imagined this seldom worked. The troops were rarely able to advance as rapidly as had been predicted due to mud, barbed wire, underbrush and the fresh shell holes left minutes before by the advancing barrage. Thus, the troops would fall farther and farther behind the advancing barrage, giving the enemy time to return to their senses, come out of their bomb shelters and get themselves and their machine-gun and artillery crews ready for the approach of the lagging troops. Again, there was simply no way to communicate to the artillery that they needed to slow down the pace of their advance.–ed.)

Waited about all day. News of our advance is encouraging. Several persons were brought in. *(presumably to train the troops in the use of unfamiliar equipment which was arriving in large quantity.–ed.)*

A vast supply of unfamiliar grenades and pyrotechnics arrived. As the battalion filed by at dusk, an officer stood at the roadside explaining their various purposes and methods of functioning, and expounding, like a patent-medicine artist at a fair, their many sterling qualities.

"This one will call down a friendly barrage in your front; you better take a couple. This one will indicate your position to a passing aeroplane, works equally well by day or night, every soldier should have one (wait till the plane circles about and drops six white stars). This will burn through flesh and bone and provide a high quality of illumination for night attacks (may be thrown by hand or from the rifle). And here is one (with apologies for the fact that it weighs ten pounds) that will destroy man and beast within a radius of forty yards (pressing it into the arms of some bewildered soldier)," and so on till his voice was lost in the darkness.

Friday Sept 27

The bombardment started at 2:30 A.M. of the twenty-seventh with a roar stretching from horizon to horizon, and the upper air grew alive with whistling sounds; on the high ground in front the shock of explosions merged into one deep concussion that rocked the walls of the dugouts.

Our artillery was supposed to have blown a passage through the heaviest wire between some craters marked on the map, but there didn't seem much chance of locating it by sense of touch. I found myself groping over something like the surface of the moon. One literally could not see two yards, and everywhere the ground rose into bare pinnacles and ridges, or descended into bottomless chasms, half filled with rusted tangles of wire. Deep, half-ruined trenches appeared without system or sequence, usually impossible of crossing, bare splintered trees, occasional derelict skeletons of men, thickets of gorse, and everywhere the piles of rusted wire. It looked as though it had taken root there and it was so heavy that only the longest-handled cutters could bite through it.

Rained all day, No messages.

When the occupation of the front was complete,
runners were sent to report it to Battalion Headquarters; and perhaps half of them succeeded in
reaching its location, but none succeeded in ever
returning to their companies. *(half the runners killed
on the way to deliver the report and the other half killed
on the way back.—ed.)*

Our boys are still advancing.

I figured that we had gone nearly a mile forward
without meeting any Germans save two or three
killed by shells; the fog was as blind as ever, and
we hadn't an idea of what was happening on the
ridges to either flank. So we slipped and slid down
to the valley bottom and were met with automatic rifle fire from the farther crest. I told Lieutenant Rogers to try out those new model ther-
mite rifle grenades on them, but nothing occurred. I didn't discover until afterward that the
detonators came in separate boxes.

Saturday Sept 28

At dawn of the 28th, the two battalions took up
their slow and groping progress across the ridges.
The ridges were cloaked in a dense growth of
small trees and the bottoms choked with underbrush; it was seldom possible to see over twenty
yards, often not five. Each opening through the
leafy wall was a death trap. There was rifle fire
from across the narrow valleys—it needed but a
few men to do it, well hidden in chosen spots,
and looking for a glimpse of khaki among the
green or the shaking of bushes.

There was a slow steady drain of casualties, with never a blow to be struck in return, and oh, the long weary way those wounded had to travel back.

Rained all night but managed to keep dry by stretching my shelter half over me. Nothing to do but hang around.

It was a ghastly night of uncertainty and sudden alarms, of bursts of fire coming from none could say where, of hunger, and of long, long hours of drenching darkness.

Sunday Sept 29

On the twenty-ninth little or no progress was made.

Very little doing here. Our advance continues.

Monday Sept 30

Nothing to do but rest. Rained all day.

By the afternoon of the 30th, it was evident that the enemy position was being evacuated, and the two battalions were deployed in double line for a concerted assault behind half an hour's artillery preparation. This artillery preparation had frankly become a thing to dread. There was no direct observation of their fire, due to the blind character of the country and the still apparent lack of aeroplanes; nor was there any direct communication from the infantry units to the batteries. If a platoon or company were suffering from the fire of their own guns, they could send a runner with a message to that effect to Battalion Headquarters, perhaps half a mile or more distant through the woods; and Battalion Headquarters, if their wires had not been blown out, would communicate with regimental headquarters, who in turn would take it up with the artillery; and the artillery would quite likely reply that the infantry were mistaking enemy fire for their own.

Tuesday Oct 1

Nothing doing all day.

At early dawn of October 1st, the advance was resumed, and by evening, after one and a half kilometer's slow advance, the leading elements had encountered another position of organized resistance. It was fronted with strong wire and heavy machine-guns, and was not attacked in force on that day.

Rode to Florent{*sic*} in a truck and saw a good show given by our divisional troop this evening.

Wednesday Oct 2

Spent a cold night. Frost on the ground when I awoke. Prepared to move. Boarded lorries at 1:30 P.M. Moved up about 10 K. into the woods.

At three A.M. Captain Blagden came into the old German dugout where I had been sleeping to tell me that we were to attack behind a rolling barrage on the front at six. I remember that my teeth were chattering so with cold that I could hardly answer him. A ration party brought up some stew and coffee from the depot before we started, but not enough for every man to have some of both. They rose shaking with cold, from the half-frozen mud of an old trench and stumbled numbly forward through a forest white with frost.

This place was occupied by Germans before this drive started. They have a wonderful system of dugouts. Some are made of concrete. All are built well enough to spend a winter in. I occupy one with eight other men. We have a stove, table & chairs as well as a cot for each of us. We have two windows and a door.

For some in the support companies it had been a night of strange luxury in the German bungalows; the comfort of cots, blankets, and stoves, of strange pink bread, tasting of malt, and of apple jam.

All the comforts of home.

Thursday Oct 3

Our artillery was enough to cover an advance, but certainly not to destroy any wire; from somewhere in front came occasional bursts of machine-gun fire and the sound of bullets striking the tree trunks around us. I sent back a runner, a red-headed Irishman named Patrick Gilligan, to hurry forward my rear platoons, and had just gotten word to the others to be ready for an instant advance in open order, when the shelling started. Nothing seemed to be falling short, but it was all beyond the barbed wire. We moved forward from our trench to the edge of the barrage line, a brigade attack consisting of two lonely platoons. I was thinking of the letter of a would-be suicide once published in the papers ending: "Good-by old world, good-by," and I wondered whether my men realized what they were up against.

The barrage was stunning to watch for those twenty minutes, there within forty yards of it— the thick smoke among the leaves, the black fountains of earth, and the great yellow trees crashing down in front. Then it ceased, and at once the whole forest began to echo with a sound like a hundred pneumatic riveters at work. We moved forward into a close wall of foliage, combed and re-combed by the traversing bullets, and we fired blindly into the leaves as we went. The noise was deafening. Then Gilligan returned with the other two platoons and saluted with a grin. I told him I thought that we had lost him.

"Never fear Captain," he answered, "and praise God it's here that we are and in time for it all, and yourself so safe." And even as he spoke he was down with a bullet through the brain.

Nothing to do but toast bread.

Friday Oct 4

(This was the last day of Sgt. Horn's battalion being in the relatively quiet divisional reserve position. Although they would move closer to the front along with their battalion headquarters, they were still in reserve.–ed.)

Usual snap to-day but all good things must end. We were notified that a guide has come to take us back to our Batt as we are no longer in Div. Ris. We will not leave until to-morrow morning however.

By dusk of the 4th, we had reached the crest of a plateau, but with the loss of a battalion commander, all three company officers, and an unknown number of men. Lieutenant Rogers, the last of the three to be hit, had crawled forward alone some two hundred yards along a shallow ditch, in an effort to locate the enemy machine-guns, and in so doing had passed over the bodies of two others who had apparently died in the same endeavor. Within thirty yards of a machine-gun in action his knee was half shot away by a sniper even nearer to himself; and under this point-blank fire he managed to free himself from his pack, get a tourniquet on his leg, and crawl backward to the company, which he outposted and put in position for defense. A lieutenant from the 308th, was then put in command of the company, but was in turn wounded. Captain Grant of Company H was now the only senior officer left in the battalion and started forward to take command of it, but, before reaching the front, was killed by a shell, which also mortally wounded his only lieutenant. Lieutenant Jenkins, in command of Company E, now found himself in command of the entire Second Battalion. That night the troops huddled into such shelter as they could find, while the enemy artillery blasted the valley from end to end.

Sat Oct 5

Started after breakfast and hiked until about 4 P.M. stopping at our kitchen for a bite & some mail at noon.

Toward noon of October 5th the brigade commander, coming up on the ground, found the troops under Lieutenant Jenkins withdrawing from a seemingly hopeless position and ordered another general assault. The companies and battalions were by now thinned and merged beyond definition. New lieutenants, coming up from the rear as replacements, were put in charge of whatever elements were at hand and launched upon whatever attack was under way. Officers returned wounded to hospital never knowing with what troops they had fought, and the men moved to obey their orders half-drugged with exhaustion.

We are to remain at Batt Hdqtrs & act as runners. Jerry paid us a visit at dusk and dropped a few bombs.

The attack ran afoul in the acres of barbed wire and it got no further. The main hope lay in an infiltration along a ditch next to some railroad tracks where a platoon was sent to crawl in single file along the bottom. When the last had disappeared around a slight bend along the way, the battalion commander followed to watch their progress. They now all lay in sight of him, and only one was yet alive, shot through the legs and returning with his rifle the fire of a machine-gun in position upon the tracks, till another burst of fire from it tore him to pieces. So the attack failed.

Sunday Oct 6
An eventless day.

An attack at early morning on the sixth and continued by steady pressure throughout the day,
advanced the line only slightly beyond the position held four days before, and did little more
than move the field of operations to that point.

Monday Oct 7

Our Batt Hdqtrs moved up a bit. Placed on relay post
between 1st & 3rd Batt.

At dawn of the seventh the attack was resumed,
and by noon the enemy showed the first signs of
withdrawal.
Moving under a constant machine-gun fire, and
cutting its way through the wire, the battalion at
length reached a position of vantage. They advanced in single-file along a winding trail, an in-
effective fire passing overhead. It was done almost without loss; yet to those who knew him
the death there of Sergeant Watson marked the
advance with loss enough. He had pushed out to
locate a machine-gun firing from the flank, and
fell shot through from the shoulder to the hip.

Rained hard and received a good drenching.

On October 7th an American soldier captured
while on patrol, was returned with a written de-
mand for surrender. The message was English,
on clean paper, and had been written on a type-
writer, something which certainly could not have
been produced by any American Battalion on the
line. It was courteous to the verge of being flow-
ery, a point worth mentioning because the rumor

spread among the men that it was very blood-
thirsty in character. On the contrary it began by
commending the messenger with the assurance
that he had been captured through no fault of
his own and had shown himself to be a brave
soldier. It then went on to state that relief by
their comrades was clearly impossible, that the
crying of their wounded was distressing to hear,
and that in the name of humanity they would do
best to surrender. No reply was ever returned.

Tuesday Oct 8

Moved up again this A.M. Our boys are making good
progress.

At daybreak of October 9th, now with a new colonel, the regiment had pushed forward, against a
delaying fire of machine-guns and artillery, some
five kilometers. For the first time in nearly three
weeks, it had briefly emerged from that never
ending forest into open grass-lands.

Waited around while it rained and then moved forward
again late in the P.M. Had three slices of bread to-day. One
for each meal. Slept in a German hut.

Wednesday Oct 9

Awakened at 5 A-M- and prepared to move. Cold & chill
to the bone. Frost on the round. Moved forward at 6 A.M.
Traveled over hills & valleys, through thick woods until 8
P.M. We have pushed forward about 7 kilos. Slept in a batch
of woods while bullets were whizzing through the air & shells
falling near us.

Thursday Oct 10

Awakened at 3 A.M. to meet some rations comming{*sic*} up. Ate a light breakfast and prepared to advance again. Moved ahead a short distance & remained there all day while the 153 Brig. passed us & continued the push. After waiting on line at the Reg. mess for 3 hours I was out of luck for eats & had to be content with a slice of bread. Groped my way back in the dark & went to sleep.

Friday Oct 11

Awakened at 3 A.M. & joined the scouts who preceded the Batt. Placed at a cross road to act as guide. When my Reg. had passed I started to rejoin my unit. Had a long walk. Located them late in the P.M. Slept in a German hut. My sleep was disturbed by heavy shelling & strong counter attacks by the cooties during the night.

Saturday Oct 12

Did not advance to-day. Expect relief to-night. Heavy shelling during the day & night.

Sunday Oct 13

Shelling is so severe that we were compelled to seek shelter & remain under cover most of the day. In charge of a ration detail this P.M. Served a hot meal. The first in three days. Was out with a recononance{*sic*} patrol at night. Wandered all over no-mans land & worked in conjunction with a party of engineers who were to throw bridges across the Aire River[65].

An attempt by a patrol of Company D to cross
the river on a broken bridge had been repulsed
with loss, nor had the other patrols along the
banks discovered any fords; an attempt by the
engineers to throw bridges across at night had
also been driven off by artillery and machine-
gun fire.

Very dark night. Returned about midnight. Sleep disturbed
several times by shells bursting close by & forced to seek
shelter.

Monday Oct 14

Aroused at 5 A.M. by heavy shelling from the enemy.
Reached the dug out in the nick of time as some shells dam-
aged the shack a bit. Several men being injured. Heavy artillery fire all day. Prepared for a good nights rest. Shells were
bursting close all night and was compelled to spend most of
my time dodging in the dugout. Received no sleep at all.

Tuesday Oct 15

Ordered to prepare to move after breakfast. We are to
advance once more. Our hdqtrs have been moved forward.

On the morning of the fifteenth, a general assault was ordered. Morning broke with a thick
white mist clinging over the open meadows, and
blotting out the town of Grand Pré beyond the
river. At six-thirty the American artillery opened
fire upon the wooded hills, and an hour later the
First Battalion advanced to the attack. Despite
the protecting fog, the first movement of troops

into the open brought a sweeping fire of artillery
and machine-guns from the high ground and from
the north bank of the river.

Communication has been lost between one of our Co. &
Hdqtrs. I was chosen to go with another man & locate it. We
crosed{*sic*} through thick woods to avoid observation. By the
aid of a compass we finally pushed our way in the correct
direction to the end of a clump of woods. We had to cross an
open space. This we did by crawling part of the way & dashing the balance. Machine gun bullets whizzed close to us but
we were not hit. Reached the R.R. track in the valley and
located our company. We delivered our message and returned
safely.

Four successive messengers sent out to this platoon from the company P.C. at the railroad station had been shot before reaching it, but without deterring the fifth from going, or from continuing to go.

Moved forward again and dug in the side of a road.

By two P.M., under a constant storm of 77 and 88
millimeter artillery shells and machine-guns,
which had already caused the casualties of an officer and sixteen men, Company C built up its
firing line along the south bank of the river. Company D held the railroad tracks behind it. Company B, having also consumed the forenoon in its
gradual advance, had carried its firing line first
to the tracks by the railroad station, and thence,
by infiltration, to the trees and bushes of the
river, where three platoons lined the banks, while

the fourth huddled down in support along the
concrete platform of the railroad station.

Went out on a ration detail and did not return until dark.
Our boys tried to advance several times but were held by
heavy machine gun & artillery fire. They managed to reach
the outskirts of Grand Pre{*sic*} towards evening however. Our
hdqtrs moved up during a downpour of rain and spent the
night at the R~R. Station. We expect relief to-night. Rain
continues and sleep is impossible.

Wednesday Oct 16
Our boys entered the town at dawn and took the enemy
by surprise.

Just as the first gray streaks of dawn began to
appear we started cleaning up the west end of
the town. Taken completely by surprise, the
cleaning up of the town was accomplished with
astonishingly little loss. Not a shot had been fired
nor had any sentinel been met when, still in complete darkness, a single figure came around the
corner of a building; there was a startled *"Mein
Gott"* and still in silence, with the muzzle of a
pistol at his stomach, the first prisoner had been
captured.
He told of a garrison of one-hundred fifty in the
town, all machine-gunners or automatic-rifleman,
and led the way to the cellar occupied by the
rest of the squad. At his summons they climbed
out, their packs on their shoulders, and were
passed along to the rear.

We captured about 100 prisoners and 15 machine guns. Our relief was on its way while we were establishing our new line. The enemy is shelling us heavily and we wish that relief would hurry. Our only protection is the side of the buildings.

> The American soldiers were flattened against the sides of the buildings, when a German officer passed. He seemed to be leading out a relief of the guard, and all might have filed on into an ambush had not someone shouted "Hands up." The officer swung around, falling as he did so with a bullet through the neck. Some of the German soldiers he was leading were shot as they ran; a few were killed in the street, and some more made prisoners; but probably the greater part escaped.

Shrapnel is flying dam{*sic*} close. The man next to me saved my life but lost his own by stopping a piece of shrapnel with his head and killed him almost instantly. He spilled his blood & brains all over my equipment & part of my clothes. I left them all behind when we were relieved about two hours later.

> The relief by the 312th and 311th Infantries of the 78th Division began on the night of the fifteenth through daybreak of the sixteenth. The ground of the First Battalion was not taken over until one P.M.

Was sent on to our kitchen & received a hot meal. We had to walk through heavy mud for about 5 miles to reach them. Slept in an old German baloon{*sic*} shed which protected me from the heavy rain during the night.

The taking of Grand Pré represents probably the most successful action of the regiment, for it is the only occasion on which it can fairly be said that the enemy was driven *en masse* from a position which they had fully intended to hold. Such occasions are much more rare than might be supposed, even in the course of a long and eminently successful, advance. The war, as it was found by American troops, seems very seldom to have involved a fight to the finish on any one bit of ground; and the most that was usually accomplished was to hurry a withdrawal that the enemy would have done at a later date. The casualties of the regiment for this accomplishment were twenty-four killed, ninety-one wounded, seventeen missing, and seven gassed, one hundred and thirty-nine in all.

Thursday Oct 17

Breakfast at 6 A.M. started on our march to the rear at 8:30 A.M. Stopped at the roadside at 11 A.M. for mess and continued at 12 N. The roads were covered with a heavy thick mud deeper than our shoe tops. The passing trucks splash us with mud and we were one mass of mud when we stopped for the day at some German shacks and put up for the night. We covered about 15 kilos. Rejoined my company to-day.

During the sixteenth and the seventeenth the regiment was withdrawn seven kilometers to the south, and then thence on the next day as far to the southeast. Here a collection of German huts and barracks, ranged one above another on a slope, gave lodging to the whole command, and here for four days the regiment remained, resting, bathing and refitting.

Friday Oct 18

Rested all day. Checked up on equipment. Am recommend for a sergeancy{*sic*} and am acting as such.

Saturday Oct 19

To-day shall go down in history. We took our first bath & were deloused since early in July. Received entirely new clothes & blankets. Slept as sound as a bell without my cootie friends to disturb me.

Sunday Oct 20

Rained all day. Remained in the hut to keep dry.

Monday Oct 21

Our drill schedule started to-day. We marched to some field about a kilo away through heavy mud. I took charge of my platoon but did very little work on account of the poor condition of the ground. About 10:30 A.M. an order to prepare to move was issued. We marched out at 1 P.M. The movement is a mystery. No one knows where we are bound for. Hiked about 8 kilos back towards the lines. After crossing fields full of shell holes and dead Germans we were ordered to dig in at the side of a hill.

On the twenty-first we moved north about six kilometers to a line representing the Corps line of resistance where, for four days they garrisoned and, which was actually more truly the case, dug

the trenches. On the twenty-fifth the battalions were returned to there previous positions where they received replacements, five hundred for the regiment, and remained in rest and training for the rest of the month.

We are about 3 kilos from the front line. It is becomming{*sic*} dark and impossible for our kitchens to prepare a meal so we went without supper, to sleep.

Tuesday Oct 22
Up at 7 A.M. Numb with cold. Ordered to make up baffle packs and prepare to move. Hiked 2 kilos to our kitchen and had a light breakfast. After about 2 more kilos hike we stopped where some engineers were at work and our company was put to work digging trenches. Finished by about 3 P.M. It was dusk when we returned. Retired to my funk hole after mess.

Wednesday Oct 23
My appointment to a sergeant was announced this morning. Hiked to the same place we dug trenches yesterday and resumed our work. It is a clear day and the planes are very active. Two of our baloons{*sic*} & one plane were brought down. Towards evening Jerry sent over quite a number of shells. He had obtained the range of a nearby French Battery and the shells were screeching overhead.

Thursday Oct 24
Hiked again this A.M. and dug more trenches. After our days work we hiked all the way back to those German shacks

and arrived there at dusk. Am tired & exhausted. Retired at 6 P.M.

Friday Oct 25
Took things easy to-day.

Saturday Oct 26
Followed a schedule of drill to-day. Retired early.

Sunday Oct 27
Drilled as per schedule.

Monday Oct 28
Practised{*sic*} aviation signals asisted{*sic*} by an aeroplane. Drilled this afternoon.

Tuesday Oct 29
Drill this morning. Aviation signalling{*sic*} this afternoon. As we returned we noticed a sign on our shack "Mumps. Keep Out". There had been four cases of mumps amongst our residents so we were notified that we were in a class by ourselves and that we were not to mingle with the rest of the common herd. In other words we are quaranteened{*sic*}.

Wednesday Oct 30
The "Mumps" gang went out for a short hike. And some physical drill in the fields this A.M. Rested the balance of the day.

October 31st began the final phase of the 307th Regiment's role in WWI. After advancing through the Argonne Forest, they successfully took control of the town of Grand Pré. Now the final advance was begun north to the river Meuse where there would be one last encounter with the Germans before the end of the war. The Central Powers began to fall with Turkey surrendering on October 31st, 1918, followed by Austria on November 3rd, 1918, and finally Germany at the 11th hour of the 11th day of the 11th month of 1918.

Mr. Horn was taken out of action on November 1st due to influenza. He was taken fifty miles south to Base Hospital #9. He was rejoined with his regiment on December 20th at the Chaumont training camp. Brief accounts of what he was missing will be presented for the days of his absence.–ed.

Thursday Oct 31

(Armustice{*sic*} with Turkey)[66]

Rolled our packs early this morning and moved out at 8:45.

> On the morning of October 31st, the 307th Infantry was moved from its billets six kilometers north. Its orders were to follow, at about two kilometers, the rear elements of the 153rd brigade.

Hiked about 8 kilos with full equipment and was all tired out when we arrived at our destination which was a high hill.

> On the last day of October, the division again resumed the front occupying the same ground it had held when it was relieved, the high ground north of Grand Pré. Very little progress had been made north of Grand Pré during their two week respite from the line.

> We had to dig in. I felt pretty bad and went on sick report. I had acquired an attack of Influenza and was placed on a stretcher and in a tent. The night was very chilly.

Friday Nov 1

Remained here all day.

> Throughout November 1st they did not advance,
> for the 153rd brigade was attacking the last orga-
> nized line of enemy resistance south of the Meuse,
> and the resistance was still very strong.

After mess I was carried away in litter & placed in an ambulance. I had a fifty mile joy ride. I was bounced and jossled{*sic*} until I imagined I would be shaken apart. It reminded me of the Witching Waves at Coney Island[67]. Arrived at Base Hospital # 9 about midnight and after being registered I was assigned to a bed with white sheets and four thick heavy blankets. It felt strange to lie in a bed once more. Spent a restless night. Perhaps because I am not accostomed{*sic*} to such comfort.

Saturday Nov 2

> By morning of November 2nd this line had been
> broken, and the troops started forward on a long
> advance, an advance such as had never before
> during the war been opened to Allied troops, and
> which in five days should carry them, half fam-
> ished and wholly exhausted, across thirty-eight
> kilometers of enemy territory to the river.

> At dawn of the second, the regiment advanced
> across the Aire where, in a single group, lay eighty
> of the enemy's horses, killed by shell-fire. The
> first battalion was loaded on trucks and, pushing
> north, the trucks of the First battalion reached
> Thenorgues. Perhaps due to the rumble of mo-

tors in the street, or perhaps by chance, the enemy began a heavy shelling of the town, and the troops were withdrawn to the woods, where, after an advance of over 10 kilometers, they took up positions a little before dawn.

Rested all day while it rained. Feeling very bad to-night. About 10 P.M. I was taken out on a litter and placed on a Red Cross Train. Pulled out about midnight.

Sunday Nov 3 (Armistice with Austria)[68]

Am on a French Hosp. Tr. and have a frenchmen{*sic*} as an attendant to get our food and take care of us. Each car is divided into compartments. There are only two men & the attendant in mine. We have about 35 patients on this car. Rode all day. My pains are gradually leaving me. It began to rain again towards dusk. Stopped at Allcry (*?–ed*) about 9 P.M. and was carried to Base No. 26 where I was given a bath, a suit of pajamas and placed between two white sheets again. Slept fairly well. Occassional{*sic*} fever.

Toward noon of November 3rd, the advance was resumed past battered houses still burning in the rain. There had been intermittent shell-fire through the night and morning which grew to such intensity as to force a halt. And while they halted here, waiting for the shelling to cease, there passed overhead, like flocks of wild geese, squadron after squadron of aeroplanes, hundreds of allied planes, and the sky seemed black with them. Then came the continuous roar of their falling bombs. Whatever there was of enemy strength or munitions marked for destruction, its destruction must have been very complete.

At 11 P.M. orders were received to take over the front at dawn and the regiment again started forward. The roads were deep in mud and crowded with traffic and, as almost always at night, it was raining.

Monday Nov 4

More rain. Feel pretty good this morning. Am well taken care of and have sufficient to eat. Remained in bed all day. Examined by the doctor.

Dawn of November 4th revealed an open ridge a mile to the north pitted with machine-gun positions. The first forward movement of troops brought a sweeping fire from these positions across the front where two enemy field guns also went into action. Fire both from machine-guns and artillery was too intense to attempt a frontal assault across the intervening valley.

Our accompanying guns were close behind, and a message to them brought a very prompt fire on the positions across the valley—a fire in which our machine-gun company also joined. The front line troops filtered down the slope but they could gain no ground up the farther slope. The fire on both sides was extremely heavy; the crew of one of the American field guns was wiped out by a direct hit, and in the course of the day the two leading battalions lost four officers and some sixty men.

Tuesday Nov 5

Remained in bed & rested.

At day break of November 5th, after a further shelling of the ridge opposite, the Regiment again started forward. Pushing north against artillery fire, across country, and constantly urged to speed, the units began to lose cohesion. The enemy could be seen drawing off across the open hills to the northwest. Our machine-gun company, which had been carrying its guns by hand, and continued to do so without losing distance during the succeeding days, opened with effective fire on these targets. In front, on its commanding hill-crest, rose the town of Stonne, and toward this goal the advance continued.

Upon entering, the town was found to be filthy with a litter of garbage and refuse strewn broadcast about it; and packed in the church and the graveyard was a crowd of civilians, gathered together for their hour of deliverance. As the first American troops came down the street, close along the house walls, in one tide of hysterical joy they streamed forth to greet them. Four years of bondage, in hatred and in fear, and these were their deliverers, a people whom they had never seen before, but had been taught to love, and the French do not try to conceal emotion. Old men, old women, and girls, their arms were around the necks of the soldiers, and their poor pillaged homes were ransacked for some token, some hidden treasure of food, to press, laughing and crying, into the hands of the hungry and tired men. It was worth much of hardship and of suffering to have been among the first troops into Stonne; not often is the fruit of victory spread at one's feet in such a harvest of human hearts.

The enemy, still on the outskirts of town, were firing down the streets. A patrol of eight men, two from each platoon, under Lieutenant Hoover and Sergeant Cook, the latter already twice evacuated for wounds on other fronts, and who, as platoon leader, was intended to have gone himself. They had completed their route without any losses, and had returned to the edge of town when, for one fatal moment, they gathered at a crossroads in the darkness and driving rain; and a single shell, striking fairly in their midst, killed or wounded every man. Only one was able to walk back, badly wounded, to the company with the news that the sergeant and four others were killed, and the lieutenant mortally wounded.

Stonne too had been heavily shelled by the enemy, and a number of the civilians wounded, while others, their brief rejoicing over, moved out, pushing their scant belongings before them in wheel-barrows, into the night and the rain.

The night was one of drenching rain, of exhaustion, of hunger, and of confusion.

Wednesday Nov 6

Rested all day. Rained again.

6:15 A.M., November 6th.—No rations arrived as yet.

With or without rations, at six-thirty A.M. of November 6th, again the advance started. Pushing north the two leading battalions were met, on the northern edge of the woods, by heavy machine-gun fire. Artillery preparation was called for and this was delivered in upwards of an hour's time, together with fire from the machine-gun company; but the operation occupied the entire forenoon.

Standing on the open slope one could see the enemy streaming back over the bare hills and our advancing skirmish line and artillery columns. It was a beautiful motion-picture of well-ordered war, but there was no contact between the two; the Germans did not wait for that. Yet had it not been for a somewhat academic insistence upon artillery preparation, there might well have been contact. All troops were halted for upwards of an hour, while a total of seven shells was thrown at a supposed machine-gun position while the enemy made good their escape.

At 4:15 P.M. the first troops of the brigade reached the river Meuse. It was everywhere evident that the enemy had just left.

Thursday Nov 7
Read in Bed all day.

On the afternoon of the seventh an attempt was made to build a bridge across the river. A covering party was sent to aid in this operation. They were soon engaged in a fight with enemy machine-guns on the farther shore; and, though the latter seemed at the end to be silenced, the engineers had lost one man wounded, and the covering party had one killed and seven wounded, and the work on the bridge was discontinued.

There was shelling of Remilly *(a small town on the Meuse—ed.)* throughout the day, with the pathetic killing of a few civilians—poor worn women, who had bravely endured four years of bondage and oppression, to die in the hour of their deliverance and at the very close of hostilities.

Friday Nov 8

Still in bed. Rain again this evening.

Throughout the eighth, enemy shelling continued. There was little or no response, for, due to the condition of the roads and the rapidity of the advance, the American guns had not yet caught up.

Saturday Nov 9

Doctor issued orders that I may recieve{*sic*} my clothes. However I remained in bed all day.

On the ninth, a sergeant and six men from Company F completed a footbridge at Remilly and crossed to the north bank of the Meuse at three A.M. A patrol of the sergeant and two of his men crossed the bridge over the Meuse at six forty-five A.M. and went forward about one hundred meters unmolested.

Sunday Nov 10

Still waiting for my clothes. News that the Kaiser has abdicated[69].

Heavy shelling of the towns and cross-roads continued with projectiles varying from three to nine inches in caliber. The surgeon of the First Battalion had been killed while at work in the dressing station, and a single shell had wiped out the driver, five horses, and the rolling kitchen.

Monday Nov 11

Not feeling so well to-day. Learned that the armustice{*sic*} has been signed by Germany at 5 A.M.[70] this news reached the hospital wild shouts of joy could be heard as the news spread from ward to ward. Those who were well enough joined the mob which was forming to parade over the area to give vent to their feelings. They used dish pans for drums and their voices could compete with any brass band.

The American artillery, now in position, was firing, but not heavily, and with strangely restricted targets. First it was ordered that they should avoid firing upon the towns across the river, then that they should also avoid the crossroads, then the cultivated fields; and finally came a strange and incredible rumor that an armistice was to be signed and that all fire should cease. Yet 11 A.M. of November 11th brought to that sector no sudden or dramatic silence of the four years' thunder of the guns—no outburst of rejoicing, nor any friendly greeting of old enemies. One might wish that it had, but it did not. There had been very little firing through the morning, and after eleven there was none. The ancient women, who had trundled out of town their wheelbarrows, loaded principally with nondescript bedding and still more ancient women, reappeared at once trundling them back again. And for the rest of the troops, smoking the last of their tobacco, waited more hopefully, but quite inarticulately, for better rations.

Tuesday Nov 12

Moved into the main ward with orders to remain in bed.

The first thrill of victory came on the twelfth, when a French battalion in new uniforms, with colors flying and music playing, with the song of victory in their step and the light of it in their eyes, their officer flashing his sword on salute at their head, came swinging through the streets. It was the first glimpse any had had of the pomp and circumstance of war, and formed a delightful memory of its close.

Mr. Horn appears to have remained in limbo until December 20, 1918 when he rejoined his regiment at Chaumont. It was a pleasant limbo filled with days of relaxation and sight seeing. For the rest of the regiment things were a little more difficult.—ed.

There were the long leagues of muddy roads, back across the old battlefields and through the old ruins, and still on over a country untouched by war; till, in the first day of December, they reached a more or less permanent station near Chaumont. There for five weeks they drilled, deloused, and equipped, but mostly drilled. To many it seemed that they drilled too much, for it was six hours a day and, on orders from high authority, "regardless of the Weather". Yet one who undertakes to disregard the weather of Northern France in winter is undertaking much, and it is more easily done in the office than in the mud. Then, too, the minds of all were filled with but one thought: "When are we going home?" . The war was over, and it was an effort of mind that anything else should matter.

Wednesday Nov 13
Clear cold day. Feeling much better but must remain in bed.

Thursday Nov 14
Still in bed & resting well.

Friday Nov 15
Still in bed.

Saturday Nov 16
Same as yesterday.

Sunday Nov 17
Dido{*sic*}

Monday Nov 18
Dido

Tuesday Nov 19
Signed the payroll

Wednesday Nov 20
Received my clothes and left my bed. Felt good and thought I would walk about 10 miles. Changed my mind after taking a short walk and returned to my bed exhausted. Had my first glimse{*sic*} of the Hosp. & grounds and reminded me of Camp Upton & those stump pulling days. This is the

biggest hosp. camp in France. Consisted of nine base hosp. I was so tired that I slept through the night without arousing once until morning.

Thursday Nov 21

Visited a barber to make myself presentable for my homeward journey which I hope will be soon. Took a stroll visiting the village of Allerey*(?–ed.)* It is a very small place. The inhabitants have erected small stands similar to those at Coney Island. These places are always crowded by convelesant{*sic*} soldiers eager for some eatables. They pay exhorbitant{*sic*} prices for things. But in our eagerness to obtain these luxuries we allow ourselves to be robbed. These are a few examples of the price charged Fruit bar (5c value) 2 Francs (4Oc) 3 apples 1 Fr. (2Oc) Bar of Choc (10c value) 3 Fra (60c) Thin slice of cheese not enough for a sandwich 1 Franc Small can of jam 7 Francs

Friday Nov 22

Took my daily walks and retired early.

Saturday Nov 23

To-day was pay day. We received our usual pay of 45 Francs. Applied for a pass to Chalons[71] but was told no more would be given until Tuesday.

Sunday Nov 24

Spent a quiet restfull{*sic*} day.

Monday Nov 25

Took a long walk this morning. Am regaining my strength rapidly. Visited the dentise{*sic*} and had my teeth examined. Obtained a pass for *{nothing written here in the actual journal but judging from the entry of November 26, it was probably the pass for Chalons-sur-Marne that he could not obtain on November 23.–ed.}*

Tuesday Nov 26

Hurried to the R.R. station immediately after breakfast. Bearly{*sic*} had time to catch my train after having my pass recorded & purchasing a ticket for Chalons. The fare is 6c. The distance is 18 kilos. Arrived at Chalons about 10 A.M. Walked up the main Boulevard and into a bank. Had 2 of my express money orders cashed and became 109 Fr. richer. Met a friend from my ward. And we spent the day together. After walking around town and seeing whatever proved interesting we entered a restaurant and ordered a Table de Thate[72] dinner which set us back 4 Fr. With the addition of a few drinks of vin rouge our stomachs seemed satisfied. We walked some more after lunch and I make a few purchases. We visited a few more cafes and nearly missed our train back at 5:30 P.M. Returned to camp at 7 P.M. Retired early.

Wednesday Nov 27

Performed a sad operation to-day. Shaved off my moustache which had stuck to me through all my battles and hardships. Buzzed it with military honors.

Thursday Nov 28

Celebrated Thanksgiving Day with a good dinner which consisted of turkey & dressing, mashed potatoes, corn, pudding, nuts, figs & apples. Never ate as much since I am in the A.E.F.[73]

Friday Nov 29

Examined by the major and was placed in A. class. Will soon be leaving the hospital.

Saturday Nov 30

Rained most of the day. Remained indoors & read.

Sunday Dec 1

Spent a quiet day and enjoyed our usual Sunday dinner of chicken, etc.

Monday Dec 2

Just taking things easy. Waiting to learn what they intend to do with me.

Tuesday Dec 3

Same as yesterday.

Wednesday Dec 4

There is an epedemic{*sic*} of scarlet fever in Camp. Several wards are under quarantine. Our throats are examined every morning. I am becoming so lazy that I have my breakfast served in bed and don't get up until about 10 A.M. We had our nightly "barrage" after the lights went out and when we should be in dreamland. Mockasins{*sic*}, pillows, towels, socks, magazines & newspapers filled the air. I had to seek shelter under my bed from the flying {*sic*}, exposing myself only long enough to get a shot at some innocent, slumbering patient. We agreed to an armistice about 11 P.M. Hostilities will be resumed to-morrow night.

Thursday Dec 5

Nothing new to relate.

Friday Dec 6

Applied for a pass to Chalons for to-day.

Saturday Dec 7

Arose at 7 o'clock. Washed, shaved, ate a hurried breakfast and caught the 8:40 train to Chalons. Arrived about 9:30 A.M. and walked through the town and was grately{*sic*} interested and at times, amused by the costoms{*sic*} & habits of the populace. Enjoyed a delightfull{*sic*} dinner at the Hotel Modern. After this we continued our sight seeing and made a few purchases. We visited a few popular cafes. Ate supper at the "Cafe de la Gare"[74] and made my train in time. Returned to camp at 7 o'clock tired & sleepy. Retired early.

Sunday Dec 8

Had a wonderful night's sleep. After being aroused & served my breakfast, I turned over and slept some more until 10 A.M. Enjoyed my chicken dinner & took things easy the rest of the day.

Monday Dec 9

Nothing new.

Tuesday Dec 10

My division has sent out a call for all Class A convalescents. Expect to be on my way soon.

Wednesday Dec 11

Passed the physical examination by the major this A.M. After dinner was ordered to get my things to-gether{*sic*} and be ready to move to the convalescent camp. It is raining and the ground is terribly muddy. The C.C. is only across the R.R. tracks and I was comfortably settled in my tent at 2:30 P.M. This tent accommodates a platoon of me. Even has an army cot, a straw mattress & 5 blankets. Am in the 1st Platoon of F. Co. Had a good supper. Still raining. The only thing to do is "hit the hay". Fell asleep as soon as my head hit the pillow.

Thursday Dec 12

Answer to the call of reville{*sic*} for the first time in 5 months. Still raining. No drill this morning. Visited the old ward and stayed with the boys all morning. At 1 o'clock we had to answer the fatigue call. I was placed in charge of the mess to carry a car load of wood for the kitchen.

Friday Dec 13

Slept well last night. Visited M. ward after mess breakfast and stayed until retreat. Returned to the ward to spend the evening playing cards with the boys. Rained all day.

Saturday Dec 14

Haven't heard when we are to leave yet. Spent the day at the ward with the boys. Returned early and "hit the hay".

Sunday Dec 15

Sunday is like every other day in the army, we attended the flag raising exercises at the administration building just before retreat. Still tramping in mud. Retired early to give my shoes & socks a chance to dry.

Monday Dec 16

Same as usual.

Tuesday Dec 17

Spent the A.M. at the ward. Was ordered to remain in the immediate vicinity ready to be evacuated & issued a blanket. After supper went over to the ward and saw the movies at the Red Cross Hut with the boys. Bid my friends goodbye & retired early.

Wednesday Dec 18

Ate an early breakfast. Ordered to pack up. Assembled at the drill grounds, with other men of my division at 9:30 A.M.

After standing around for about an hour in a drizzle of rain we were informed that our train had pulled in and departed. We are to return to our quarters and await further orders. The army is still as dizzy as ever. Rained all day & night. A strong wind is blowing and it seemed as if the tent might be blown away several times during the night.

Thursday Dec 19

Up at 5:30 A.M. Ate an early breakfast. All 77 Div. men were ordered to report at the drill field immediately after breakfast with all their belongings. At 8:30 A.M. we had a roll call and marched off behind the camp band to the R.R. station. Our train did not arrive until about 11 o'clock. We piled in those 8 Cheveaux or 40 Hornmes pullmans. I was fortunate to get on a 3rd class coach. Stopped near Dijohn[75] about noon and received our iron rations for the day. A French troop train had stopped on the next track. Our boys who detest "canned willy"[76] were swaping{sic} their rations with the "Frogies"[77] for sardines etc. I guess they have the same opinion of sardines that we have on corned beef. We stopped again at , <italic>{this was a space here in the journal. The writer probably was going to inquire as to the spelling of a town's name and neglected to add it.}<italic> an American supply base. The Amer. Red Cross gave us some coffee & bread. We are still riding late at night.

Friday Dec 20

Arrived at Cheaumont[78] at 7 A.M. A distance of about 60 miles from our starting point. It took us just 25 hours to get here. We were lead to French Barracks to rest until transportation could be had to take us further. We have orders not to leave and a guard was posted to see that this is enforced. I sneaked out and located a Y.M.C.A. and purchased some buiscuits{sic}. My first bite to-day. Entrained at 1 P.M. and rode 13 kilos to Bicon[79]. Given a cup of coffee and placed in barnes{*sic*}. Will continue to our companies to-day. Made a soft bed of hay and had a good nights rest.

Saturday Dec 21

After a breakfast of coffee & bread we were separated according to the regiment we are in. There are 55 from the 307th. At 8:30 A.M. We marched off under the command of an officer. We hiked 16 kilos to La Ferte sur Aribe[80], where our 2nd batt. is located. Had more coffee & bread. It is now 2:30 P.M. After a short rest, the men from our batt continued to Lanty a distance of 7 kilos more. Arrived at the company at about 5 P.M. Mess had been served. All that was left was some soup & bread. Am more tired than hungry and was satisfied. Met some of the boys and were glad to see each other. It feels like home to get back. After a few drinks at the estimate I was invited by my pass to sleep at a French house with them where they slept. We have a wonderful little room with two double beds. They are high wooden beds. I almost sank to the floor in the soft mattress. Had a wonderful nights sleep.

Sunday Dec 22

Rained all day. Nothing to do but rest. Walked to the next town of De Trutyville*(?–ed.)* and listened to a band concert this P.M. Spent awhile at the estiminete{*sic*} after supper. My pal Ben Weher drank a little more than he could hold. I took him back early. Undressed him & put him to bed like a child. We had a lot of sport with him. All quieted down towards midnight and we fell asleep.

Monday Dec 23

Started for the drill fields at 8:30 A.M. It had rained all night and increased in the fury, while we were on our way.

Received orders to return to our billets and drill in our quarters until the rain subsided. Rain continued all day therefore remained indoors all day.

Tuesday Dec 24

Drill from 8:30 to 11:30 A.M. in solving a tactical problem. Close order from 1:30 to 3:30 P.M. More rain this evening and during the night.

Wednesday Dec 25

Went to the bath house which is built in a barn, with five other men. Built a fire, heated the water and took a bath. Eleven of us had arranged a Christmas Dinner & Supper with a French Family. We had "beaucoup" wine & eats and enjoyed same immensely. We furnished our own entertainment and had a wonderful time. We had also made a collection for the children of Lanty. We gave an entertainment & chocolate & Buiscuits{sic} to the kiddies. Every man was presented with tobacco & cigars which they value highly and certainly showed their appreciation. The entire town Folk turned out for the celebration which took place in an old Chateau{sic} during a heavy rain. We had our first snow fall this evening. The trees, houses & the ground is covered with white snow which adds to make this Christmas day realistic.

Thursday Dec 26

Owing to the heavy snow fall, we are drilling indoors this morning. There will be no drills in the afternoons of any day between Christmas & New Years. Spent the afternoon lounging about. Retired early.

Friday Dec 27

Drill this morning in the snow covered fields. Transferred back to my old Platoon and drilled with them. Dried my shoes & socks this P.M.

Saturday Dec 28

Inspection this morning. Rained during the day as usual. An order came through that I am to attend an infantry school. Will leave here Jan. 2. Lounged about all day. After an evening in the esteminate, I retired to my downy bed.

Sunday Dec 29

Rain again! Our company took over the guard for the town. I am sergt. of the guard and am responsible for its care. Why even the mayor of this berg is under my jurisdiction. Inspected the posts about 10 P.M. & retired.

Monday Dec 30

Made a couple of tours of inspection and turned the guard over to Co. B. at 3 o'clock without any mishap. More rain as usual. Spent the evening at the esteminet and retired early.

Tuesday Dec 31

Drill this morning. Was told to be ready to leave for school to-morrow at 5:30 A.M. Will accompany the Captain. Still raining so I spent the afternoon writing letters. The esteminet had orders to remain open 12 M. this being New Years Eve. We were having a good time until the Madamme{*sic*} who owns the place discovered that six bottles of champagne were missing and unaccounted for. This announcement created quite a disturbance. Not being one of the guilty party and having no desire to be mixed up in the scrap, I "partir tout suit" [81] and went to bed.

Wednesday Jan 1

Awakened at 4:30 A.M. Breakfast at 5 A.M. Left for Deuteville[82] with Captain Palmore and some men who were on their way to Aix Le Bain[83] on leave. Mounted a lorie{*sic*} and waited at Chateaux Villian*(?–ed.)* for the captain to arrive in a rig with his baggage. The captain after receiving his traveling orders got an auto to drive us to Chaumont. Stopped off at Bricon{*sic*} to get a steel helmet. Arrive at Chaumont about 12 N. Our train does not leave until 6:40 P.M. so we were allowed to visit the town. There are only five from our Reg. going to school (2 Captains, 3 sergts.). We three Sergts. strolled around to-gether. After a hearty meal we wandered around town. Ate supper at the buffet near the station. Just had time to meet the captains and get aboard the train.

Thursday Jan 2

Got off at Curcy Le Tour *(?–ed.)* at 6 A.M. and waited until 7:53 A.M. for a train to take us to Ciamercy[84]. Had a cup of coffee at a cafe near the station in the meantime. The passenger place on this train was limited and we were compelled to ride in the baggage car. Arrived at Ciamercy{*sic*} our destination, at about 12 N. We made our way to the Hdqtrs. of the 3rd Army Corps school, through a shower of rain. After registering we were directed to the adjutant of the Infantry weapon School. He was out to lunch which reminded us that we were hungry. Left our luggage in his office and hunted up a place to eat. Partook of a light lunch. Returned to the adjutants office and were assigned to barracks. We were shown a diagram the location of the camp. It looked like a swell place on the blue print, but when we found the place it was nothing more than a mud hole. We picked our bunks and wished to wash up. Upon inquiring for the bath house, that we noticed on the blue print, we were told it has not yet been built and that the only place to wash is in the canal about 1/2 kilo away. We waded through mud to wash in the canal and waded back again, Returning dirtier than before. We went back to town as quickly as we could get away from that muddy place. Located a French family who obliged us with some supper. Had a few drinks and waided{*sic*} back through the mud and crawled into our bunks. I am so tired that I had no trouble to fall asleep although the place is as cold as a refrigerator.

Friday Jan 3

Too cold to get up from under the warm blankets. Missed breakfast. Arose at about 9 A.M. Washed and shaved. School does not commence until Monday. Drew 2 blankets, a rifle, belt & bayonet from the 2 M. for use in our course. Almost drank more than I could hold at the esteminet this evening. The law to close at 8:30 P.M. was the only thing that saved me. Retired feeling extremely happy.

Saturday Jan 4

After breakfast I strolled to town. Visited the ancient cathedral which was built in the 8th century. Climbed 23 steps to the tower from which I attained a wonderful view of the town. Had my photo taken minus my moustache and hope it be a better likeness of myself than the one I had taken at Chalons Sur Soam[85]. Although the sun shone for a while this morning the rain broke through for another sucessful{*sic*} attack upon the soil of France this P.M. Took in the movies at Y.M.C.A. this evening. Heavy rain during the night.

Sunday Jan 5

Attended the first formation here at 8 A.M. The rules and regulations were laid down to us and we were told that the opening of school was postponed until Wednesday. We must attend two formations daily until then one at 8 A.M. the other at 1:30 P.M. Last nights heavy rain caused the Seine River to swell. The streets of the town are flooded and the inhabitants fear a repetition of the flood of 1910. Our bath house & guard house were washed away by the overflow. The boys were all hoping our camp would also be destroyed so that we could return, but no such luck. Great quantities of lumber came floating down the river in its mad rush to the sea. Some of the old folks were scooping it up to put in a supply for the winter. I watched them and soon joined in the sport of diving for wood. We thought it was a great sport and helped the old folks at the same time, to their satisfaction. Two other sergts. and myself had arranged a supper with some French Folks and reported at the appointed time at 6 P.M. We enjoyed our chicken, etc. After spending a pleasant evening we waided{*sic*} through the mud & water to our barracks and hit the hay at 9:30 P.M.

Monday Jan 6
Formation at 8 A.M. & 1:30 P.M. Took a short hike in the afternoon for about 8 kilos & returned tired & hungry. Received our daily rain.

Tuesday Jan 7
Was assigned to the Musketry Course this P.M. Rained a bit. Took a walk about town. Was fed Corned Willie three times to-day. So we ate supper with a French family.

Wednesday Jan 8
School opens to-day. Up at 6 A.M. Breakfast at 6:30. First formation at 7:30 A.M. Divided into platoons of representative divisions. Marched to Hotel De Ville and attended a lecture until 10:30 after which we marched to the training grounds and received instructions in sighting. Returned in

time for dinner and had a tactical problem to solve between 1 & 4 P.M. Unable to shave or wash until after my day work.

Thursday Jan 9

Lecture before our mornings work. Rained all morning. Lecture & instruction on gas this P.M. Skipped the lecture scheduled for this eve. to take a stroll before retiring.

Friday Jan 10

No rain to-day. Old Sol surprised us by staying with us all day. Rifle practise{*sic*} this morning. Tactics this P.M. Stopped at a French family, had some hot chocolate and ordered a dinner for Sunday Eve.

Saturday Jan 11

Rain the early part of the day. The Sun paid us another visit about 11 A.M. Same schedule as yesterday. After supper saw a good entertainment at the Hotel De Ville.

Sunday Jan 12

Raining heavily. Did not get up until 10 A.M. Enjoyed a big dinner and while lieing{*sic*} down to digest my meal I fell asleep. Slept all P.M. Enjoyed that supper with the French folk which was arranged earlier in the week.

Monday Jan 13

Spent the entire day in securing a clean outfit and bath to rid myself of my bosom friends the cooties. Promenaded this eve. and retired early.

Tuesday Jan 14

Spent the morning at the rifle range. Captured five machine guns in our tactical exercises this P.M.

Wednesday Jan 15

Shot at the R.R. while it rained. Slept through the aftnoon{*sic*} lectures at the conference hall. Saw some movies at the Y.M.C.A. It is a beautiful moonlight night and enjoyed a short stroll before retiring.

Thursday Jan 16

This is a beautiful day, I can't remember the last time that the sun shone so bright and the sky was so clear. Shot at the range this A.M. Drew some more clothes this P.M. Enjoyed the amateur show at the town hall this evening, selected from talent amongst the students.

Friday Jan 17

At the range this A.M. Lectures on Patrols in the conference hall this P.M. Took my usual evening stroll before retiring.

Saturday Jan 18

At the range this A.M. Listened to a talk on Liaison by aviators who had worked with our division and helped locate the "Lost Battalion".

Editor's note- The Lost Battalion *is worthy of mention. Among World War I aficionados, the story of the 308th is well known. On October 2nd, 1918, Companies A, B, C, H and G forming a battalion of about six hundred men from the 308th Regiment, found themselves surrounded by the Germans on about a 400 yard area of slope between the Moulin des Charlevaux and the Bois de la Buironne. Here they remained trapped for five days until October 7th when they were liberated by members of the 307th regiment. During this time they had no food and water was only obtained at great risk to life from a nearby stream. The Germans continually tried to destroy or capture these soldiers with flame throwers, machine-gun fire and shelling. The Americans were valiantly able to defend themselves but at great cost. Of the original six hundred men, about three hundred survived, the others succumbing to starvation, infection and death under fire. There is an interesting anecdote to this period which demonstrated a measure of compassion on the part of the Germans perhaps mixed with a show of respect:*

A single soldier creeping down through the bushes to fill his canteen at the stream where the bullets were constantly splashing, was shot through the leg and disabled. There a squad of the enemy found him, dressed his wound with care, and offered him his choice of being carried back with them as a prisoner or left to be found by his friends. He chose the latter, and was known to his party as their best-bandaged casualty.

Early to bed.

Sunday Jan 19

Paid my captain a visit this A.M. Found him still lieing{*sic*} in his bunk. Had an interesting conversation in which we discusted{*sic*} the possibility of our early return to the states. We had already imagined ourselves back when some one entered with a grunt, "Damn this mud hole", and we realized we were still at Clamecy. Visited the aeroplane hangers this P.M. and recognized many of the planes that flew over our div. while we were in Argonne. They had the statue of Liberty our Divisional Insignia painted on them. Sat in one of the observers seats to notice how it feels but I guess one must fly through the air at the rate of about 125 miles an hour to get the real sensation.

Monday Jan 20

Troubled with a bad cough all of last night and went on sick report. I happened to have a high fever and I was tagged for the camp hosp. Took my personal belongings and piled in the ambulance at 7:45 A.M. After a speedy ride, I was registered and assigned to bed 17 Ward C3. I lost no time to get into a clean suit of pajamas and between the white sheets again. I am not really sick but I managed to dodge the exams that take place to-day & to-morrow. Spent a restful{*sic*} day.

Tuesday Jan 21

Have my meals brought to me and enjoy all the comforts of life. Read about every magazine in the ward.

Wednesday Jan 22

When the doctor asked me how I felt this morning. I told him I am through "gold bricking" and ready to get back to school. You see the exams are over now. Sure enough I was given my clothes and given my walking papers and moved back to the barracks. Retired early.

Thursday Jan 23

It feels good to get back on the job. Shot on the range and received our usual boring instructions from young Bob Fitzimmons. Chase all over the fields this afternoon solving some tactical problems. Saw a real good show at the town Hall given by some traveling troupe.

Friday Jan 24

This is a cold day. The temperature has fallen steadily all this week. Shot on the range this A.M. Tactical problems in conjunction with the aeroplanes this P.M.

Saturday Jan 25
Shot exceptionally well this A.M. receiving 42 out of a possible 50 at 500 yds. Tactics this P.M. Cold weather still continues.

Sunday Jan 26
Busy cleaning up this A.M. Took a stroll this P.M. Coldness subsiding and slightly snowing toward evening.

Monday Jan 27
About 3 in. of snow on ground. Continued to shoot well on the range this A.M. Had a test on some tactical problems in the conference hall this P.M.

Tuesday Jan 28
More snow during the night. It is now about a foot high. Did more shooting this A.M. during a steady snow fall{*sic*}. Lecture this P.M.

Wednesday Jan 29
Drilled in the snow all day.

Thursday Jan 30
Same as yesterday.

Friday Jan 31
Same as yesterday.

Saturday Feb 1
Took the final examinations and feel confident that I passed this A.M. Finished the coarse this P.M. An exhibition was given by one of the platoons for the colonel. Our platoon was selected to work the targets in the pit for them. It was announced that by taking an average of the shooting of all

the students attending the school that the average mark qualified us as sharp shooters. My platoon compromised of men from the 77th & 81st Div. won the pool for the best shooting of the N.C.O.'s. My score was 232 out of a possible 300 which is a little below the average.

Sunday Feb 2

Took my weekly bath and also shaved. Yes. I am finally getting accostomed{*sic*} to a bath as often as this. Strolled about town and retired early.

Monday Feb 3

We begin a two days maneuver to-day. Left the drill grounds at 7:30 and hiked about 4 kilos to our starting place along a steep hill. The zero hour was set at 9:30 and promptly at that time our artillery, machine guns, 37 men & stokes mortars[86] opened up with as pretty barrage as I ever heard. We advanced along the valley and around the hill, crossed a pontoon bridge that the engineers had constructed and advanced under cover of the barrage. By combining fire and movement we finally made our way to the top of Beaumont Hill, which was our objective. When we made our final stand everyone was shooting at the dummy targets. A Flock of about 25 quales{*sic*} strayed in our field of fire and all took the concequinces{*sic*}. Many of the boys will have quale{*sic*} of toast to-night. About two hours of the P.M. was spent discussing this morning's problem and listening to a lecture on machine guns. Early to bed as usual.

Tuesday Feb 4

Continued yesterdays attack and captured the hill this A.M. Cleaned up my equipment this P.M. and turned same in this evening. Received my clearance slip and am ready to "partir"[87] early to-morrow morning.

Wednesday Feb 5

Awakened at 4:30 A.M. Ate an early breakfast and formed according to divisions. We were issued individual traveling orders and piled into those Box Car Pullmans. The train left at 8 A.M. Had to jump around the car like a jack rabbit to keep from freezing. Arrived at La Roche[88] about 10:30 A.M. and a few of us got off and inquired when the train left for Paris. None was due until 4:30 P.M. so we visited the town. It is a very small place and the esteminate was about the only place we could spend our time. We met a few interesting people there . Went through quite an experience when the train pulled in on time there was so big a crowd waiting for it that the only place I could find was in the baggage car and that soon became filled to its fullest capacity. We had a jolly crowd there however and we soon forgot our discomfort by singing & joking. Arrived in Paris at 7 P.M. Had to wait on line about 45 minutes to register. Was only allowed to stop over night and have to catch the 8 A.M. train out to-day. Of course I was disappointed but I must make the best of it. A Y.M.C.A. man met me and placed us in an auto truck after a long wait the truck was loaded to the brim and we were off to the Rochester Hotel[89]. We road{*sic*} through the Concorse[90]. It sure is a beautiful place. All sorts of cannon were lined up on both sides of the street. Upon our arrival at the hotel we registered and were assigned to beds for a payment of two francs. The building is a dandy and was probably occupied by some wealthy people "avon la guerra"[91]. After we were settled we hired a taxi and told him to drive us where there was some life. He left us out on Boulevard De La Madalaine[92]. We promenaded about and never before did I see so many 'Madamoiselles"{*sic*}. There sure were "beaucoup". Spent a good deal of the time riding around in taxis. I don't remember the time that I returned to the Hotel and rested my weary bones.

Thursday Feb 6

Up at 6 A.M. Restaurants are closed. After a good wash & shave prepared to leave. Hailed a taxi I wouldn't attempt to ride on the "Metro", for fear of losing myself and rode to the station. Upon our arrival we asked the driver "Combien"[93]? He said nothing. We insisted that he name his price. He said he would leave that to us. One of my friends broke his heart and gave him 1 franc. We must have traveled quite some distance too. We "checked out" and received transportation to Chaumont on the 8 o'clock train. We traveled second class. We made good time and arrived at 12 N. The train to Bricon{*sic*} does not leave until 5:43 so we ate a hearty dinner and strolled around town. We returned to the station early and met a truck that was going to Div. Hdqtrs. To save time we got aboard. Arrived in Chateauvillian *(Seems to be the same place he refers to on January 1 as Chateaux Villian—ed.)* about 6:30 P.M. I reported to the Town Mayor who fixed us up with a place to sleep. We are so tired that we retired early.

Friday Feb 7

Up at 7:30 after a good nights sleep. Breakfasted at the Casual mess and were soon on our way again. It had snowed all night and still continues. No trucks are going our way so we must hike to our company. I have 15 kilos to go. It was far from being pleasant while trudging through the snow. Finally arrived at the company at 12 N. just in time for dinner. I was welcomed with the good news that we are preparing to move Sunday night. Which soon made me forget that I was tired. Spent the afternoon lounging around drying my wet shoes & socks. The company clerk drew my money for me while I was away and I received five months back pay amounting to 921 francs. I had great difficulty to find a place to sleep. I finally located a downy bunk. (down on a hard stone floor) and "coucher"[94] for the night.

Saturday Feb 8

Sat around the fireside most of the day. It is becomming{*sic*} cold again and the roads are slippery. One of the boys was ordered to report to Battalion Hdqtrs and left a nice bed with a "canopey"{*sic*}. I lost no time in taking advantage of this opportunity to make myself comfortable and spend a good nights sleep.

Sunday Feb 9

Arouse{*sic*} at 7:30 A.M. Rolled my pack after breakfast and am ready to move at a moments notice. Left Lanty *(?– ed.)* at 9 P.M. Hiked to Latracy *(?–ed.)*, 12 kilos on a very slippery road and many spills were taken. It is a very cold night. Arrived about midnight. We were served hot coffee and stew before we entrained. Thirty-three of us were piled in one of those side-door Pullmans. It is very fortunate that we have plenty of hay or I believe we would freeze.

Monday Feb 10

We did not pull out until about 3 A.M. We are so crowded that we cannot be flat on the floor. We have bread & "Canned Willy" to last the trip but no one cares to eat any. Although the cold weather continues, our crowded condition enables us to keep warm.

Tuesday Feb 11

The gang's still here and as crowded as ever. It looks as if we must spend to-night in this car.

Toward the middle of February came the next stage of the long trail home, when the last battalion of the regiment moved out at night, under a cold half-moon, company after company in dim silhouette of packs and rifles, black against the moonlit ice, with the calling of good-byes behind, and twenty kilometers of glare ice in front—that and a four hour wait at dawn for a train unheated, in numb and bitter cold. The war was not over with the signing of the armistice.

Wednesday Feb 12

About 8 A.M. we stopped at Sable{*sic*}[95] and gathered the information that this will be our Division Hdqtrs. and that we will be in this area.

In the Embarkation Center at Sablé life became pleasanter, for there the spring was already beginning.

Rode on to Poilli{*sic*}[96] where we detrained and hiked 8 kilos to Auvers Le Hannon *(?–ed.)* and was billited{*sic*} in a Chateau{*sic*} just outside of the village. We are billited according to platoons. Some boys drew some nice sleeping quarters. I will sleep in a corner of a garret in the barn. The weather is warmer here and no sign of snow. The cooks had only time to prepare coffee and "Canned Willy" so a couple of the boys & myself went into the village to try our luck for "eats". After inquiring in several places we finally struck a place where we could get some potatoes. The woman was so busy waiting on soldiers that we had to fry the potatoes ourselves. We sent to the butchers for some meat and also cooked that. We succeeded in making a good meal and soon was my old self again. I got my allotment of straw and made myself a good bed on the floor in the comer of the garret in barn.

Thursday Feb 13

Just walked around to get aquainted{*sic*} with the place and retired early.

Friday Feb 14

Rained to-day and the drill schedule which was to start to-day was postponed. Played a sociable game of poker this evening and was set back 100 francs when I quit and retired.

Saturday Feb 15

Inspection this A.M. Took things easy the balance of the day.

Sunday Feb 16

Slept all morning. Rained and spent most of the time indoors.

Monday Feb 17

Our schedule of three hours drill in the A.M. & 1 hr atheletics{*sic*} in the afternoon started to-day.

> There was continued drilling, but less of it, continued delousing, and more of it, equipping, some excellent baseball, and innumerable inspections, which quite definitely required a black and brilliant polish on shoes which were frankly intended to be rough and brown.

Went to town had a few drinks and retired.

Tuesday Feb 18

Same schedule as yesterday. Battalion review was held at retreat.

Wednesday Feb 19

No drills. Rain all day. Payday.

Thursday Feb 20

We were to hike to Sable to hold our Div. Review but owing to the inclimate{*sic*} weather and to our complete satisfaction it was called off. Drill as usual. The fields are in muddy condition.

Friday Feb 21

Drill as usual. Still raining. Sergt's meeting this evening to discuss the affairs of the company and of our captain. Early to bed.

Saturday Feb 22

Inspection this A.M. The sun & rain alternated all day. Bought some eggs & meat and had a French woman cook us a supper.

Sunday Feb 23

Heard the rain patter on the roof so I slept all morning. Had supper with the French family and attended a concert given by A Co. this evening. Retired 10:30 P.M.

Monday Feb 24

Awakened at 5 A.M. Ate an early breakfast and formed at 7 A.M. Hiked 16 kilos by a round about way to the Divisional Review grounds near Sable and arrived there about 1:30 P. M. We were lined up in our Divisional formation

> It offered a most magnificent spectacle, massed upon the field in lines of battalions formed in close column of companies at one-half normal distance, showing with their steel helmets and

> fixed bayonets like some great Roman testudo or
> Macedonian phalanx of gleaming metal, a mighty
> and resistless engine of war

and waited until about 2 P.M. when we were inspected and received by Gen. Pershing.

> On February 24th the 77th Division was reviewed
> at Solesme by General Pershing. It had been re-
> viewed at Florent just three months previously
> by General Alexander, but this latter occasion
> seemed more notable.

Several officers & men were decorated with the D.S.C. Gen Pershing delivered a complimentary address

> The Commander-in-Chief made a remarkable
> statement. So remarkable was it in fact that, for
> fear of misquotation, one almost hesitates to set
> it down. For he said:
> "I consider the 77th Division one of the best—in
> fact it is, in my estimation, *the* best division in
> the A.E.F."
> It is a distinction which, of course, every self-
> respecting division both claims and proves; but
> one can only assume the verdict of the Com-
> mander-in-Chief to be final.

after which we passed in review and lined up for a cup of coffee. We had our daily rainstorms. Started back about 4 P.M. by the same rout{*sic*} and reached our billets about 8 P.M. where we received a well deserved supper. Tired and aching feet. Retired early.

Tuesday Feb 25

No drill to-day. Slept until about 8:30 A.M. Learned to my surprise that Capt Hastings had died early this morning, believed to be of a broken heart. Every one in the Co. is sad and gloomy. The Chaplain administered the ceremony at 2 P.M. The entire company paid their respects to the captain as his body was taken away. More rain to-day.

Wednesday Feb 26

Drill this A.M. Our Batt. Athl. meet was held this P.M. Our Co. carried off the honors receiving 52 out of 110 points. We also won the competition for the best drilled platoon. Our third platoon excelled. A notice was posted on the bulletin board giving Gen. Pressings' remarks concerning us. It reads as follows. "In inspecting this company on Monday Feb. 24 the Commander-in Chief made the following remarks: "A fine body of men, Splendid personel{*sic*}. It is my wish that the 77th Div. shall be the best division that ever marched in N.Y. City. It's fighting record is unsurpassed and it is the duty of every officer and soldier now in the division to make its appearance worthy of the fighting record"

Thursday Feb 27

During drill this A.M. we had some batt drills. I was in charge of my platoon which we assumed was a company and I acted as Company Commander. It was interesting and I must admit that I am surprised no buttons poped{*sic*} off my blouse from the swelling of my chest. Games in the P.M. Strolled to town this eve. Retired early.

Friday Feb 28

Muster occupied the entire A.M. Games this P.M. My request for a pass to Paris was returned disapproved. Rain again.

Saturday Mar 1

Up at 4:30 A.M. Formed at 6:30 and hiked 12 kilos to Fontaine[97] where we held a regimental review. Our third Platoon competed for the best drilled platoon in the reg. but did not win. At noon we were given 1/2 cup of coffee and with the sandwich that we brought along comprised our dinner. We held our inter Battalion Athletic meet this afternoon. Our Batt. won easily. Our company scored the greatest number of points.

In March there was a military and athletic meet of all the divisions in the Embarkation Center, which the 77th Division won, and in which Company H of the 307th won both the platoon and company drill competition for all these divisions.

Hiked back and reached our billets about 6:30 P.M. After supper I retired.

Sunday Mar 2

Slept all morning. Our new Capt. Palmore joined our company this day. The clock was set ahead an hour by order of the Div. Commander. Put in a request for a pass to Nantes. Wrote letters this P.M. Same changeable weather still continues.

Monday Mar 3

Rain again. No drill.

Tuesday Mar 4

Drill this A.M. My pass to Nantes is approved and takes effect to-morrow. Passed the physical exam this P.M. before going on leave. Formal retreat.

Wednesday Mar 5

Ben Weber & myself started off about 8 A.M. on our leave of absence for 14 days. Hiked to Sable and reached there 10:30 A.M. We drew our ration money amounting to 45 Frcs. Was introduced to some of the Argonne Players and had lunch with them. Met Arthur Jacobson for the first time since he left Camp Upton. Boarded the 12:57 train. Changed at Angiers[98] and tried to stop over by the M P's would not allow us. Caught the 2:06 train & arrived at Nantes about 4:00 P.M. "Registered in" and strolled up town. Met some fellows we knew who advised us to stop at the Hotel Voyageurs. Washed up and ate supper at the Red Cross Rest Station where we received a good meal for the reasonable sum of two francs. We visited a few cafes, met a few friends from our division and retired to our soft bed about 10:30 P.M.

Thursday Mar 6

Up at 7:30 A.M. after a good nights sleep. Breakfasted at the A.R.C.[99] Visited a barber. Took a bus to the R.W. Camp *(?–ed.)* where we went to deliver a letter from a fellow in our comp. to his brother. We learned that he had left for the states last week. We returned in time for lunch. Met one of my nurses who had treated me in the hospital. She is homeward bound. Visited the art museum and enjoyed the paintings and statuary. Spent the balance of the P.M. at the Y.M.C.A. Dined at the A.R.C. Promenaded in the eve. and retired to my downy bed about 10 P.M.

Friday Mar 7

Awake at 10 A.M. Lounged around all morning in the hotel lobby. Purchased some post card views of Nantes and spent the P.M. sending them to my friends. Kept an appointment for 8 P.M. with a madamoiselle{*sic*} and spent a pleasant night.

Saturday Mar 8

Up at 8 A.M. After a visit to the P.S. called for my friends and had breakfast to-gether{*sic*}. Spent the balance of the A.M. in a cafe. After lunch we strolled down to the Port Transbordeur[100] and rode across the river Loire on the car which is suspended from the bridge by a metalic{*sic*} curtain. We stood in front of our hotel about 9:30 P.M. and a Lieut. who was S.O.L.[101] for a place to sleep asked us if we could help him out. After inquiring at a few more hotels without any success we invited him to share our room. To show his appreciation he asked us to join him in a drink. We took him to our headquarters (Cafe La Guerre). but they were closed. We banged & banged until the Mme. came to the door. After explaining what we wanted she directed us to the side door where we were admitted. Well I wont{*sic*} state what happened but we had a hell of a time. Got to bed after midnight.

Sunday Mar 9

Arose at 8 A.M. The Lt. asked us to accompany him to the ship on which he is acting as a convoy and is laid up for repairs. It took us about 1 1/2 hrs to reach it. We spent a pleasant time on board and had some dinner Roast duck and about eight other coarses{*sic*}. Inspected the ship and made the acquaintance of the Chief engineer & the crew. Started back about 4:30 P.M. After supper we saw a movie at the Cinema.

Monday Mar 10

Slept until 10:30 A.M. Spent a day of rest.

Tuesday Mar 11

Slept all morning. Had intentions to go to the Bordeaux this eve. but we met the chief and he asked us to stay over. Saw a few boxing bouts at the K of C[102]. and retired about 11 P.M.

Wed Mar 12

Slept all morning. Rested during the P.M. I was locked out of my room to-night and it was midnight before I could find a place to sleep.

Thursday Mar 13

It was 11:30 A.M. when I arose. Lounged around all day and took in the "Marine Show" this eve. which I enjoyed immensely.

Friday Mar 14

Beaucoup sleep & rest. Saw a show at the Y.M.C.A. this eve. Retired early.

Saturday Mar 15

Intended to leave for St. Nazaire this P.M. but changed our minds and remained over. One of the boys bought a camera from a passing sailor. We walked with him to his ship too obtain a few extra films. By the way he was leading us I surmised he is not familiar with the way. It was 6:30 when we left him. Too late to get back to town and supper. A soldier saved the day for us. He became interested in our outfit and asked several questions. He wanted us to dine with him at his mess hall. He is a cook and he proved it by making a swell meal for us. We were treated fine. Returned to town about 8:30 P.M. and retired after consuming a few drinks.

Sunday Mar 16

Had breakfast served in bed & slept until noon. Attended an entertainment at the J.W.B. *(?–ed.)* this P.M. After supper we made arrangements to "partir" to Paris. Checked out and caught the 11:05 train.

Monday Mar 17

Dozed off occasionally during the night. Arrived in Paris about 7:30 A.M. It was 8:15 before we checked in. The next train to leave for Nantes is the 8:05 P.M. We were granted permission to visit the town until that time. Enjoyed a good break-fast{*sic*} at the Hotel Pavilion[103]. Roamed about the town and took in the sights. Ate dinner & supper at the S&S[104] Club where I tasted with pleasure my first ice cream soda since I left the states. Had my pass renewed until to-morrow morning. After a stroll we rode to the Hotel Rochester in a taxi. Had a bite to eat at the A.R.C. before retiring 11 P.M.

Tuesday Mar 18

Up at 6 A.M. Rode in the Metro and arrived at the wrong station. Missed my train accidently{*sic*} on purpose and was permitted to remain over until to-night. Had breakfast at the A.R.C. and spent the A.M. writing cards. Took in the sight seeing trip on the Y.M.C.A. buss{*sic*}. Visited the Notre Dame, Efel{*sic*} Tower, Palace de Justice, Napoleans{*sic*} Tomb, The War Pantheon[105] etc. and had a pleasant trip from 1:15 to 4:30 P.M. The War Pantheon is the most wonderful picture I have ever seen. Enjoyed a good supper at the Pavilion Hotel. Put another one over on the A.P.M. and will stay over until to-morrow morning. Slept at the Hotel Notre Dame[106].

Wednesday Mar 19

Up at 6 A.M. My fuelong[107] expires today. Boarded the 7:30 A.M. train at the Montparinasse[108] Station for Le Mans. And arrived at 12:45 P.M. Had a good dinner. Reported at the P.S. *(?–ed.)*. It is raining so we are hanging around the station for the 4:45 train for Sable. Arrived 8:30 P.M. After supper we visited some friends who put us up for the night.

Thursday Mar 20

Slept until 10:30 A.M. Started for Auvers[109] after a light breakfast. A Frenchman driving our way allowed us to ride in his buggy. We reached our company about 12:30. Spent the rest of the day looking up the boys.

Friday Mar 21

We had a field inspection this A.M. It rained this P.M. So we had a poker game. I won 65 Fcs. We chattered until 11:30 P.M. & retired.

Saturday Mar 22

I am in charge of the platoon to-day and personally inspected the men & their equipment this A.M. Played poker most of the balance of the day.

Sunday Mar 23

Day of Rest.

Monday Mar 24

Drill this A.M. Rain this P.M. Remained in doors.

Tuesday Mar 25

Excused from drill while I received a haircut & had my shoes repaired More rain this P.M. Took a bath.

Wednesday Mar 26
Rain. No drill.

Thursday Mar 27
Lecture this A.M. on the history of the A.E.F. Inclimate{*sic*} weather remained indoors. Saw a show at the Opera House this evening.

Friday Mar 28
Received a pass to Avais{*sic*} to visit the Dentist. Got as far as Sable and had my tooth fixed there. I was stopped on the road by Gen. Alexander[110] who asked me several questions. I answered them to his satisfaction. After asking for my name he passed on. I made a few purchases in Sable before I returned. Reached the Co. in time for supper. Retired with an aching tooth.

Saturday Mar 29
Up at 6:30 A.M. Although it is raining eleven men & myself boarded a truck for Le Mans[111] where our division is participating the area athletic meet. To-day is the last day of the meet. Our Div. ran off with the honors by a big margin. Boarded the trucks about 5:30 P.M. and arrived at our billets about 8 P.M. Retired immediately after supper. My tooth still aches.

Sunday Mar 30
Slept all morning. Spent the P.M. writing. Had supper in town. Met some of the boys and made the rounds of estiminets. Result Every body drank but me. Brought five of them back and put them to bed. Twas a tough night.

Monday Mar 31

Visited the dentist at Sable and returned in time for supper. Saw "C" Co. Show at the Opera House this evening. (Had picture taken)

Tuesday April 1

Our drill was interrupted by the announcement that there will be a field inspection this P.M. Busy gathering up our belongings and rolling packs until noon. Hiked to the Batt Drill Field with full packs. While we were opening our packs we were told that it is an April Fool joke. But no one, beside the Major, can appreciate it. Hiked back again and marched down to town for a bath. Our team beat "A" Co at baseball this P.M. Saw the "Argonne Players" this evening at the Opera House.

Wednesday Apr 2

While the Co. hiked to the Reg.[112] Review grounds I walked to Sable to visit the Dentist. Took things easy and returned about 6 P.M. This was a beautiful day.

Thursday Apr 3

This is our third consecutive day of sunshine & the ground is beginning to dry up. Drill this A.M. Field inspection (which I ducked) this P.M. Early to bed.

Friday April 4

While we were at drill this A.M. we were watched by the Brig. Gen. & the Colonel. Of course they had plenty of critisisms{sic} to make. Watched our Reg. Baseball team take a beating from the Engineers team, this P.M. Passed the evening in our usual manner and retired early.

Saturday April 5
Our weekly inspection was followed by a route march, We imagine the purpose was to soil our polished shoes and give us something to do when we get back in the form of cleaning up again. WG received plenty of exercise in a free for all baseball game this P.M. Lined up for pay after the eve. mess and feel rich again.

Saturday April 6
We celebrated the anniversary of our departure from Camp Upton by a final field inspection by the A.E.C.[113] and passed to their entire satisfaction which means homeward bound "toute de suite". Played ball this P.M. Spent a quiet eve. and retired early.

Monday April 7
Received a pass to Poilie{*sic*} to visit the dentist. When I reached there all he did was to paint my gums with iodine. For this wonderful treatment I had to hike 15 kilos. By fast walking I got back to the Co. by 1 oclock. Watched a ball game this P.M. Ate supper in town & retired early.

Tuesday Apr. 8
Physical inspection & a route march this A.M. Took a bath this P.M. Retired early.

Wednesday Apr. 9
Route march this A.M. Received a typhoid innoculation{*sic*} this P.M. Nursing a sore arm the balance of the day. Early to bed.

Thursday April 10

Spent a restless night, Rain again! Have a high fever & sore arm. Hit the hay early.

Tuesday April 11

Route march this A.M. Witnessed a ball game this P.M. Acted as Critic for our Co. Show before it is staged.

Saturday April 12

More rain! Hopefully recovered from the innoculations{*sic*}. Bunks inspection this A.M. Remained indoors this P.M. Our Co. Show played before its first audience & went over great to-night.

Sunday April 13

Slept all morning. The sun shone this P.M. & I strolled over the fields & meadows to spent{*sic*} an afternoon with nature. To bed by 10:30 P.M.

Monday April 14

Rain again. Cootie inspection by the A.E.C. Medicos at 10:30 A.M. Indoors the balance of the day.

Tuesday April 15

More rain. Packed up our "Blue" Bags. Rolled our packs. Prepared to move to-day A.M. No place to sleep for the night so we broke the lock to the parlor of the chateau{*sic*} and made a comfortable bed out of the sofa.

Wednesday April 16

On April 16th came the final move. It was full spring, and the meadows were jeweled with cowslips and violets, and the hedges were white with blackthorn—and, oh, how long ago and how un-

> taught seemed the times in Upton, when the regiment had adopted that emblem for its own—when the battalions moved out to their entraining points.

Up at 4 A.M. Made up our "Squad rolls". Policed up thoroughly. The populace of Auvers turned out to bid us Good-Bye

> At Avoise all the school children, with their teacher and village curé *(parish priest–ed.)*, lined the street to bid them good-bye, and every soldier came out with a flower in his cap or the muzzle of his rifle. The teacher had written in English on his blackboard a message of affectionate farewell, and had taught each child to know it by heart. It is worth telling such things to those who have only heard of hostility between the Americans and the French.

as we marched through the town about 8 A.M. Hiked to Sable where we were given cocoa & crackers by the Y.M.C.A. Assigned to American Box Car # 6 with 52 other men. A Hot lunch was served. We pulled about 1 P.M. Received another hot meal about 10 P.M. Spent a crowded night.

Thursday April 17
Arrived at Brest about 9 A.M. Retrained and received a meal at the Casual Camp. Hiked about 6 kilos on an up hill road to Camp Fontana[114] where we were assigned six to a tent. Our equipment inspected. I am sergt of the guard and must furnish a guard for the Batt. Received 2 additional blankets and slept well.

Friday April 18

Revielle{*sic*} at 6 A.M. Physical & cootie inspection at 9 A.M. Turned in unservicable{*sic*} clothing & received others in exchange. Pack inspection at 8 P.M. Medical inspection at 11 P.M. Rolled packs prepared for an early departure.

Saturday April 19

Up at 3:30 A.M. Finished our packs policed up. Breakfast at 5 A.M. Moved out of camp at 7 A.M. Hiked through Brest to Piers[115]. Red Cross gave us a pr socks with chocolate crackers etc in them. Boarded the Cuba which took us to where the America was anchored. We were assigned to bunks . Am in F9 section. We waited from noon until 3P.M. before we set sail.

> The Regiment sailed from Brest between April 20th and 22nd, divided into three battalions on board the *America*, the *Louisville*, and the *St. Louis*—the latter the same cruiser which had convoyed their eastward passage just a year and a day before.

It is a strange coincident{*sic*} that to-day is the anniversary of our landing on these shores and also the day we leave them. Retired early.

April 20 to 27

We gained about 1/2 hour in time each day and spent that time in sleep. We were issued a pr of Overalls in which to lie around the decks and preserve our uniforms. We have several canteens from which we can purchase ice cream crackers candies etc. Plenty of magazines can be had and most of our time is spent reading. We have band concerts at 10:30 A.M. & 2:30 P.M. Every afternoon there is some form of amusement on the lower hatch midship. We had a boxing tournament between the soldiers & sailors Tuesday & Wednesday. Honors were about even. We had wonderful weather during the trip. Only on one occasion did we have a slight drizzle of rain. The ocean was as smooth as glass most always. The meals were very good and plenty of everything could be had. We were compelled to wash with salt water and it was extremely difficult to raise a lather from the soap. Shaving was more difficult. We are sailing at an average of 400 miles a day. The ship crew published a small paper, "The America", each morning keeping us in touch with the current events. Sunday morning we were 150 miles from shore and we cut down to our speed considerably because we are not scheduled to land before Monday morning.

Monday April 28

Rose at 5 A.M. Breakfast at 6 A.M. Rolled our packs and cleaned up our quarters. We hurried so that we could get on deck and get our first glimpse at "Gods Country". As the sun rose we strained our eyes and could just see Sandy Hook[116] on the horizon. Just before pulling into the harbor, everyone was ordered below decks so that the companies could be formed. We learned that some of our relatives were on the ferry boats chartered by the Mayors Com. of Welcome and were sailing close to the ship. The men began to filther{sic} up on deck again until we were all up and taking in the beautiful sight of N.Y.C.

By the first of May the last of them had reached New York. It was different, very different from the going forth. There were excursion steamers in the Narrows <italic>*(an inlet of water connecting the Lower Bay with the Upper Bay lying between Staten Island and Brooklyn, New York—ed.)*<italic>, crowd-

ing on either side of the transports, covered with banners and placards of welcome, filled with brass bands and such fervently rejoicing people, shouting their quick, eager questions and greetings across the water. Then came the Statue of Liberty (which will always hereafter mean far more to her troops than ever she has meant before) and the strange familiar pinnacles of the city— the docks of Hoboken and Long Island City, with the American cobbles underfoot—the eager, pressing throngs, crowded behind the iron bars, their reaching hands stretched through, and their eyes bright with tears and with worship. And the troops pressed forward along the narrow ways, their heads lifted as though for crowns, and the hot blood surging around their hearts, swallowing back their tears as they looked into those wonderful adoring faces—the roar of feet, the crashing thunder of the drums, the music echoing and reverberating through the streets, and the cheering, cheering, cheering till even the music was drowned into silence.

We were shouting and exchanging greetings with our friends and relatives on the ferry. It was a wonderful sight. Words could not express the feeling of joy that was in our hearts. It all seems like a dream. We are afraid to make too much noise for fear of being awakened. We landed at Hoboken at about 10 A.M. From there we boarded a ferry boat and rode down and around Manhattan, up the East River to L.I. City. Boarded the train for Camp Mills[117]. Arrived about 6 P.M. and was met by brother Ed, Sis. Rae and Leo Susskind and was overjoyed to see them. We were marched off to camp and assigned to tents. As soon as I got rid of my pack I rejoined the folks and dined together at the Hostess House. Retired about 10 P.M.

Tuesday April 29

Remained in camp all day awaiting to be deloused. Not feeling well. Remained in my tent. Retired early.

Wednesday April 30

Awakened at 1:30 A.M. Took all our blankets & clothing with us to the delousing plant and put them through the delousing machine. Had a physical exam and a cold water bath. Our unserviceable clothing was exchanged. I received an entire new outfit. It was 5 A.M. before we were finished. After breakfast I had my clothes altered while I waited. It was afternoon when I reached the city on my 48 hour pass. Visited my former employers and met quite a number of my old friends. Spent the eve with Mrs. Berger & our family. Spent the night at Fleechmans.

Thursday May 1

Slept most of the A.M. Met some of the boys of the co. in the afternoon and took in a show. Returned to camp this eve.

Friday May 2

Remained in camp. Busy with the papers necessary for our discharge.

Saturday May 3

Home again (A.W.O.C.)[118] Saw the Giants play. Attended a Welcome Home party.

Sunday May 4

Had Dinner with the Susskinds and returned to camp by 7 P.M.

Monday May 5

Our company came into the city with full packs and marched to the 22nd Eng. Armory. We were permitted to go home must report to-day at 6 A.M.

Tuesday May 6

Left the armory at 8 A.M. with battle packs and formed at 11th St for the Parade. Started at 10:30 A.M. Up Fifth Ave to 116th St. Finished by 12 o'clock. Received a wonderful reception. Returned to the armory. Permitted to go home.

Wednesday May 7

Left the armory at 12:30 A.M. for L.I. City. Entrained for Camp Upton. Arrived about 6 P.M. Assigned to Barracks. Retired Early.

Thursday May 8

Received our final physical exam this A.M. Turned in our equipment this P.M.

Friday May 9

Up at 5 A.M. Turned in our blankets & mess kits after Breakfast. Cleaned up our quarters. Hung around impatiently until 11 o'clock. Marched off to the Q.M.[119] Received our bonus & pay due us. also R.R. fare. Marched to the R.R. Station. Received our discharge and boarded the tram for Home. Gee But its a grand & glorious feeling.

So the regiment came back to Camp Upton, where it was born, and was mustered out into the citizenship from which it came.

APPENDICES

APPENDIX I

WILSON'S SPEECH FOR DECLARATION
OF WAR AGAINST GERMANY
Address delivered at Joint Session of Congress,
April 2, 1917

I have called the Congress into extraordinary session because there are serious, very serious, choices of policy to be made, and made immediately, which it was neither right nor constitutionally permissible that I should assume the responsibility of making.

On the third of February last I officially laid before you the extraordinary announcement of the Imperial German Government that on and after the first day of February it was its purpose to put aside all restraints of law or of humanity and use its submarines to sink every vessel that sought to approach either the ports of Great Britain and Ireland or the western coasts of Europe or any of the ports controlled by the enemies of Germany within the Mediterranean.

That had seemed to be the object of the German submarine warfare earlier in the war, but since April of last year the Imperial Government had somewhat restrained the commanders of its undersea craft in conformity with its promise then given to us that passenger boats should not be sunk and that due warning would be given to all other vessels which its submarines might seek to destroy, when no resistance was offered or escape attempted, and care taken that their crews were given at least a fair chance to save their lives in their open boats. The precautions taken were meager and haphazard enough, as was proved in distressing instance after instance in the progress of the cruel and unmanly business, but a certain degree of restraint was observed.

The new policy has swept every restriction aside. Vessels of every kind, whatever their flag, their character, their cargo, their destination, their errand, have been ruthlessly sent to the bottom without warning and without thought of help or mercy for those on board, the vessels of friendly neutrals along with those of belligerents. Even hospital ships and ships carrying relief to the sorely bereaved and stricken people of Belgium, though the latter were provided with safe conduct through the proscribed areas by the German Government itself and were distinguished by unmistakable marks of identity, have been sunk with the same reckless lack of compassion or of principle.

I was for a little while unable to believe that such things would in fact be done by any government that had hitherto subscribed to the humane practices of civilized nations. International law had its origin in the attempt to set up some law which would be respected and observed upon the seas, where no nation had right of dominion and where lay the free highways of the world. By painful stage after stage has that law been built up, with meager enough results, indeed, after all was accomplished that could be accomplished, but always with a clear view, at least, of what the heart and conscience of mankind demanded.

This minimum of right the German Government has swept aside under the plea of retaliation and necessity and because it had no weapons which it could use at sea except these which it is impossible to employ as it is employing them without throwing to the winds all scruples of humanity or of respect for the understandings that were supposed to underlie the intercourse of the world. I am not now thinking of the loss of property involved, immense and serious as that is, but only of the wanton and wholesale destruction of the lives of non-combatants, men, women, and children, engaged in pursuits which have always, even in the darkest periods of modern history, been deemed innocent and legitimate. Property can be paid for; the lives of peaceful and innocent people cannot be.

The present German submarine warfare against commerce is a warfare against mankind.

It is a war against all nations. American ships have been sunk, American lives taken, in ways which it has stirred us very deeply to learn of, but the ships and people of other neutral and friendly nations have been sunk and overwhelmed in the waters in the same way. There has been no discrimination. The challenge is to all mankind. Each nation must decide for itself how it will meet it. The choice we make for ourselves must be made with a moderation of counsel and a temperateness of judgment befitting our character and our motives as a nation. We must put excited feeling away. Our motive will. not be revenge or the victorious assertion of the physical might of the nation, but only the vindication of right, of human right, of which we are only a single champion.

When I addressed the Congress on the 26th of February last I thought that it would suffice to assert our neutral rights with arms, our right to use the seas against unlawful interference, our right to keep our people safe against unlawful violence. But armed neutrality, it now appears, is impracticable. Because submarines are in effect outlaws when used as the German submarines have been used against merchant shipping, it is impossible to defend ships against their attacks as the law of nations has assumed that merchantmen would defend themselves against privateers or cruisers, visible craft giving chase upon the open sea.

It is common prudence in such circumstances, grim necessity indeed, to endeavor to destroy them before they have shown their own intention. They must be dealt with upon sight, if dealt with at all. The German Government denies the right of neutrals to use arms at all within the areas of the sea which it has proscribed, even in the defense of rights which no modern publicist has ever before questioned their right to defend. The intimation is conveyed that the armed guards which we have placed on our merchant ships will be treated as beyond the pale of law and subject to be dealt with as pirates would be.

Armed neutrality is ineffectual enough at best; in such circumstances and in the face of such pretensions it is worse than ineffectual: it is likely only to produce what it was meant to prevent; it is practically certain to draw us into the war without either the rights or the effectiveness of belligerents. There is one choice we cannot make, we are incapable of making: we will not choose the path of submission and suffer the most sacred rights of our Nation and our people to be ignored or violated. The wrongs against which we now array ourselves are no common wrongs; they cut to the very roots of human life.

With a profound sense of the solemn and even tragical character of the step I am taking and of the grave responsibilities which it involves, but in unhesitating obedience to what I deem my constitutional duty, I advise that the Congress declare the recent course of the Imperial German Government to be in fact nothing less than war against the government and people of the United States; that it formally accept the status of belligerent which has thus been thrust upon it; and that it take immediate steps not only to put the country in a more thorough state of defense but also to exert all its power and employ all its resources to bring the Government of the German Empire to terms and end the war.

What this will involve is clear. It will involve the utmost practicable cooperation in counsel and action with the governments now at war with Germany, and, as incident to that, the extension to those governments of the most liberal financial credits, in order that our resources may so far as possible be added to theirs. It will involve the organization and mobilization of all the material resources of the country to supply the materials of war and serve the incidental needs of the Nation in the most abundant and yet the most economical and efficient way possible. It will involve the immediate full equipment of the navy in all respects but particularly in supplying it with the best means of dealing with the enemy's submarines. It will involve the immediate addition to the armed forces of the United States already provided for by law in case of war at least five hundred thousand men, who should, in my opinion., be chosen upon the principle of universal liability to service, and also the authorization of subsequent additional increments of equal force so soon as they may be needed and can be handled in training.

It will involve also, of course, the granting of adequate credits to the Government, sustained, I hope, so far as they can equitably be sustained by the present generation, by well conceived taxation. I say sustained so far as may be equitable by taxation because it seems to me that it would be most unwise to base the credits which will now be necessary entirely on money borrowed. It is our duty, I most respectfully urge, to protect our people so far as we may against the very serious hardships and evils which would be likely to arise out of the inflation which would be produced by vast loans.

In carrying out the measures by which these things are to

be accomplished, we should keep constantly in mind the wisdom of interfering as little as possible in our own preparation and in the equipment of our own military forces with the duty-for it will be a very practical duty-of supplying the nations already at war with Germany with the materials which they can obtain only from us or by our assistance. They are in the field and we should help them in every way, to be effective there.

I shall take the liberty of suggesting, through the several executive departments of the government, for the consideration of your committees, measures for the accomplishment of the several objects I have mentioned. I hope that it will be your pleasure to deal with them as having been framed after very careful thought by the branch of the government upon which the responsibility of conducting the war and safeguarding the nation will most directly fall.

While we do these things, these deeply momentous things, let us be very clear, and make very clear to all the world what our motives and our objects are. My own thought has not been driven from its habitual and normal course by the unhappy events of the last two months, and I do not believe that the thought of the Nation has been altered or clouded by them. I have exactly the same things in mind now that I had in mind when I addressed the Senate on the 22nd of January last; the same that I had in mind when I addressed the Congress on the 3rd of February and on the 26th of February.

Our object now, as then, is to vindicate the principles of peace and justice in the life of the world as against selfish and autocratic power and to set up amongst the really free and self-governed peoples of the world such a concert of purpose and of action as will henceforth insure the observance of those principles. Neutrality is no longer feasible or desirable where the peace of the world is involved and the freedom of its peoples, and the menace to that peace and freedom lies in the existence of autocratic governments backed by organized force which is controlled wholly by their will, not by the will of their people. We have seen the last of neutrality in such circumstances. We are at the beginning of an age in which it will be insisted that the same standards of conduct and of responsibility for wrong done shall be observed among nations and their governments that are observed among the individual citizens of civilized states.

We have no quarrel with the German people. We have no feeling towards them but one of sympathy and friendship. It was not upon their impulse that their government acted in entering this war. It was not with their previous knowledge or approval. It was a war determined upon as wars used to be determined upon in the old, unhappy days when peoples were nowhere consulted by their rulers and wars were provoked and waged in the interest of dynasties or of little groups of ambitious men who were accustomed to use their fellow men as pawns and tools.

Self-governed nations do not fill their neighbor states with spies or set the course of intrigue to bring about some critical posture of affairs which will give them an opportunity to strike and make conquest. Such designs can be successfully worked out only under cover and where no one has the right to ask questions. Cunningly contrived plans of deception or aggression, carried, it may be, from generation to generation, can be worked out and kept from the light only within the privacy of courts or behind the carefully guarded confidences of a narrow and privileged class. They are happily impossible where public opinion commands and insists upon full information concerning all the nation's affairs.

A steadfast concert for peace can never be maintained except by a partnership of democratic nations. No autocratic government could be trusted to keep faith within it or observe its covenants. It must be a league of honor, a partnership of opinion. Intrigue would eat its vitals away; the plottings of inner circles who could plan what they would and render account to no one would be a corruption seated at its very heart, Only free peoples can hold their Purpose and their honor steady to a common end and prefer the interests of mankind to any narrow interest of their own.

Does not every American feel that assurance has been added to our hope for the future peace of the world by the wonderful and heartening things that have been happening within the last few weeks in Russia? Russia was known by those who knew it best to have been always in fact democratic at heart, in all the vital habits of her thought, in all the intimate relationships of her people that spoke their natural instinct, their habitual attitude toward life. The autocracy that crowned the summit of her political structure, long as it had stood and terrible as was the reality of its power, was not in fact Russian in origin, character, or purpose; and now it has been shaken off and the great, generous Russian people have been added in all their naive majesty and might to the forces that are fighting for freedom in the world, for justice, and for peace. Here is a fit partner for a League of Honor.

One of the things that has served to convince us that the Prussian autocracy was not and could never be our friend is that from the very outset of the present war it has filled our unsuspecting communities and even our offices of government with spies and set criminal intrigues everywhere afoot against our national unity of counsel, our peace within and without, our industries and our commerce. Indeed, it is now evident that its spies were here even before the war began; and it is unhappily not a matter of conjecture but a fact proved in our courts of justice that the intrigues which have more than once come perilously near to disturbing the peace and dislocating the industries of the country have been carried on at the instigation, with the support, and even under the personal direction of official agents of the Imperial government accredited to the government of the United States.

Even in checking these things and trying to extirpate them, we have sought to put the most generous interpretation possible upon them because we knew that their source lay, not in any hostile feeling or purpose of the German people toward us (who were no doubt as ignorant of them as we ourselves were) but only in the selfish designs of a government that did what it pleased and told its people nothing. But they have played their part in serving to convince us at last that that government entertains no real friendship for us and means to act against our peace and security at its convenience. That it means to stir up enemies against us at our very doors the intercepted note to the German minister at Mexico City is eloquent evidence.

We are accepting this challenge of hostile purpose because we know that in such a Government, following such methods, we can never have a friend; and that in the presence of its organized power, always lying in wait to accomplish we know not what purpose, there can be no assured security for the democratic Governments of the world. We are now about to accept gauge of battle with this natural foe to liberty and shall, if necessary, spend the whole force of the nation to check and nullify its pretensions and its power. We are glad, now that we see the facts with no veil of false pretense about them, to fight thus for the ultimate peace of the

world and for the liberation of its peoples, the German peoples
included: for the rights of nations great and small and the
privilege of men everywhere to choose their way of life and
of obedience. The world must be made safe for democracy,
Its peace must be planted upon the tested foundations of
political liberty. We have no selfish ends to serve. We desire
no conquest, no dominion. We seek no indemnities for ourselves, no material compensation for the sacrifices we shall
freely make. We are but one of the champions of the rights of
mankind. We shall be satisfied when those rights have been
made as secure as the faith and the freedom of nations can
make them.

Just because we fight without rancor and without selfish
object, seeking nothing for ourselves but what we shall wish
to share with all free peoples, we shall, I feel confident, conduct our operations as belligerents without passion and ourselves observe with proud punctilio the principles of right
and of fair play we profess to be fighting for.

I have said nothing of the Governments allied with the
Imperial Government of Germany because they have not
made war upon us or challenged us to defend our right and
our honor. The Austro-Hungarian Government has, indeed,
avowed its unqualified endorsement and acceptance of the
reckless and lawless submarine warfare adopted now without
disguise by the Imperial German Government, and it has
therefore not been possible for this Government to receive
Count Tarnowski, the Ambassador recently accredited to this
Government by the Imperial and Royal Government of Austria-Hungary; but that Government has not actually engaged
in warfare against citizens of the United States on the seas,
and I take the liberty, for the present at least, of postponing a
discussion of our relations with the authorities at Vienna. We

enter this war only where we are clearly forced into it because there are no other means of defending our rights.

It will be all the easier for us to conduct ourselves as belligerents in a high spirit of right and fairness because we act without animus, not in enmity towards a people or with the desire to bring any injury or disadvantage upon them, but only in armed opposition to an irresponsible government which has thrown aside all considerations of humanity and of right and is running amuck. We are, let me say again, the sincere friends of the German people, and shall desire nothing so much as the early reestablishment of intimate relations of mutual advantage between us, however hard it may be for them, for the time being, to believe that this is spoken from our hearts.

We have borne with their present Government through all these bitter months because of that friendship, exercising a patience and forbearance which would otherwise have been impossible, We shall, happily, still have an opportunity to prove that friendship in our daily attitude and actions towards the millions of men and women of German birth and native sympathy who live amongst us and share our life, and we shall be proud to prove it towards all who are in fact loyal to their neighbors and to the Government in the hour of test. They are, most of them, as true and loyal Americans as if they had never known any other fealty or allegiance. They will be prompt to stand with us in rebuking and restraining the few who may be of a different mind and purpose. If there should be disloyalty, it will be dealt with a firm hand of stem repression; but, if it lifts its head at all, it will lift it only here and there and without countenance except from a lawless and malignant few.

It is a distressing and oppressive duty, Gentlemen of the Congress, which I have performed in thus addressing you. There are, it may be, many months of fiery trial and sacrifice ahead of us. It is a fearful thing to lead this great peaceful people into war, into the most terrible and disastrous of all wars, civilization itself seeming to be in the balance. But the right is more precious than peace, and we shall fight for the things which we have always carried nearest our hearts,-for democracy, for the right of those who submit to authority to have a voice in their own Governments, for the rights and liberties of small nations, for a universal dominion of right by such a concert of free peoples as shall bring peace and safety to all nations and make the world itself at last free.

To such a task we can dedicate our lives and our fortunes, everything that we are and everything that we have, with the pride of those who know that the day has come when America is privileged to spend her blood and her might for the principles that gave her birth and happiness and the peace which she has treasured. God helping her, she can do no other.

APPENDIX II

PRESIDENT WILSON'S MESSAGE TO THE PEOPLE
OF THE STATE OF NEW YORK

New York's pride is in the pride of things done. Her leadership is no more due to her great wealth or her large population than to the patriotism of her citizens and the uses to which her wealth is put. In every war in which this country has engaged, she has shown a spirit of sacrifice that has made her preeminent among the States.

In this war, New York has outdone her own history.

Over one hundred and seventy-five thousand of her citizens have gone into the fighting forces of the country.

To the Red Cross, our citizens have given over thirty millions of dollars.

APPENDIX III

(Note: The following is a list of names and addresses that were found towards the back of Mr. Horn's diary, Volume 1)

Bob Marks
346 Hopkinson Ave
Brooklyn, NY

Arthur Hollander
160 Bay 31 St.
Bath Beach, NY (Bklyn)

Joe Silverman
42 Rutgets St.
NY City

Meyer Singerman
555 W. 151 St.
NY City

Mr. Chas. Bloom
230 Riverside Dr.
NY City

Mr. H.P. Reach
118-23 St.
Elmhurst L.I.

Harry Saltzman
489 Howard Ave
Brooklyn, NY

Morris Greenstein
165 E. 67 St.
NY City

Harry Bernstein
815 E 167 St.
Bronx, NY

Ed Schwartz
1735 First Ave
NY City

Philip Nerac
102 E 96 St.
N.Y.C.

E. Bilhart
1319 Hirkimir St.
Brooklyn, NY

T Winer
1275 Webster Ave
Bronx, NY

L. Glovim
1374 Boston Rd.
Bronx, NY

C. Stein
54E. 117 St.
NY City

E.C. Mosher
2027 Gates Ave.
Brooklyn,, NY

R. Reich
810 E. 6th St.
NY City

T. Wolff
68 E. 97 St.

R. Schneider
204 Ross St.
Brooklyn, NY

Miss Schley
1710 Barnes Ave
Van Nest NY

A. Lasar
1321 Hoe Ave
Bronx NY

M. Snyder
348 Manhattan Ave
NY City

M. Levin
544 St. Paul Place
Bronx NY

B. Rosen
8 W. 119 St
N.Y.C.

I. Pearl
251 So Third St
Brooklyn, NY

M.J. Roosin
143 Ave B.
NY City

D. Principe
898 Gravesend Ave
Brooklyn, Ny

B. Dobbs
133 Washington St.
Municipal Bldg Chicago Ill.

J. Hiesch
814 E. 160 St. Bronx NY

H. Bernstein c/o Meyers
92 Moringside Ave
(blank–ed.), City

M. Cohen
980 Tiffany St.
Bronx NY

A. Frank
15 W. 118 St.
NYC

Miss E. Liss
887 Faile St
Bronx, NY

Misses A & M Israel
9 W. 111 St.

A. Susskind
1321 Hoe Ave
Bronx

J. Faber
137 Fatty St
Schenectady, NY

Nat Hoffman
113 W. 113 St.

Max Weinribb
866 Beck St
Bronx, NY

L. Dubner c/o Collins
890 Fox St

Moe Drexler
1036 Simpson St

Mr. M. Orange
906 Simpson

Wm Goldenberg
956 Tiffany St

E. Zimmerman
956 Dumont Ave
Brooklyn NY

D. Schreiber
168 Lenox Ave
City
Lenox 1405

M. Taft Mysde
9345 W 189 St. Nicholas Ave

Jeff Lazarus
R60 Co. K 306 Inf.

Grossman
R4 Barrock 409.5th St.
Comp L. 306th Inf.

A1 Hirschberg
403—8th St.

B.S. Morris Roosin
411—9th St
Comp. B. 308 Inf.

L. Bloom
409—1st St

J. Seigel
P. 59

Ralph Freedman
Comp. I. 306th Inf.
R. 6

APPENDIX IV

A list of abbreviations follows with their definitions. Mr. Horn had written these in his diary as if he were taking notes for later memorization.

AM.—Amunition
C.3x Charge
C.F. Cross Firing
D.T. Double Time
F. Commence Firing
F.B. Fix Bayonett
F.L. FireLoss (from Artillery Fire)
G .Move Forward
H. 3x Halt
K. Negative (No)
P. Affirmative (Yes)
L.T. Left
R.T. Right
R. Acknowledgement
O. What is the
R.N. Range
S. 3x Support going forward
S.U.F Suspend firing
T. Target

APPENDIX V

A brief list of the members of Mr. Horn's squad.

Squad 14
Picart #1 R.R.
J. De Luca #2 R.R.
Bianco 3 R.R.
J.L. Horn Corporal

McHugh #1 R.R.
Fuchs #2 R.R.
Liebertz 3 R.R.
Wilhelm 4 R.R.

APPENDIX VI

HUMOROUS INCIDENTS

Leave it to Joe Silverman to make himself comfortable. He was lying under a shade tree in a strecher{sic} covered with a blanket to keep the flies from him, enjoying a sound sleep up the line. Max Wosling & Herman Schweitzer two descendants of German parents carried Joe off into the woods while he was asleep. They chattered away in German, arguing whether to kill him while he was asleep or to awake him & then kill him to make him suffer before he died. Joe being aroused by their noise jumped up with a start & ran like hell. You can easily get him excited by asking him how he escaped from German captivity.

Ross Williams says "We must knock the stuffings out of those Germans now or their kids will knock the stuffings out of our kids later".

Overstrom received news that his wife gave birth to a bouncing baby boy. "Gee, I'd like to see that kid" said Ovie. "You won't meet him until he's drafted in the army", said Kipp. "You've got a big job before you".

"You look sad Herbert what is your trouble" I asked. "I have a terrible pain; The doctor says I have trench mouth". What the devil is trench mouth, I have heard of trench feet & trench legs but that is a new one on me." "A trench mouth" interrupted Berry Low is one that is so large that it can hold a regiment"

One of our sergeants was overheard posting an out post on no-mans land. "This is post # 5. The enemy is practically all around you. And mind you they are very near. You must keep perfectly quiet, don't move or his snipers will surely get you. Why the men who held this post before you were all anihilated{*sic*}. Don't fire any shots or you will give your position away. If they attack in large numbers make yourself scarse{*sic*} although I don't no how the hell you can get out of this bloody hole. It is too dangerous to bring any food to you so you will have to get along the best you can until you are relieved which will be in two or three days or maybe longer if we can't get here. Well so-long{*sic*}. Be calm. You have nothing to worry about. The same sergeant after ducking a shell which had whizzed over his head. "There it goes Jim, did you see it sail through the air."

Before placing Cryan & Nunan on guard, I said "Boys, Pres. Wilson, has offered 5,000-Fr for each German you capture." During the night Nunan shouts to Cryan "Here they come, Pat, Here they come." "How many are coming" asked Cryan, "About 200" said Nunan "Sure, our fortune is made" answered Cryan as he prepared to capture the enemy.

Kupsick was found back on battalion Hdqtrs. after the raid. "What are you doing here when your comrades are fighting up front under heavy fire." he was asked. "Sir, I was also under fire. I was hiding under that stone"

Tobin & Nunan were sentries in the front line. It was a very dark night. Suddly{*sic*} Tobin whispers excitingly "Hey Nunan, Come here and hold this fellow while I call the corporal of the guard." And away he ran. After a quick examination Nunan shouted "Come back, you damn fool, its nothing but a barbed wire post"

We had hiked away from the front and had stopped over night in a village about 20 miles from the front. About 4 o'clock in the morning the blowing of a horn could be heard. It was the cows & pigs reveille. Jim Caulder jumped out of his bunk, fumbled about in an excited manner and hurriedly put on his gas mask. When told of his mistake, Jim said "Well, I don't take any chances."

Jim Caulder our cook is on duty to-day. "We'll I guess I'll make the boys a nice beef stew, with plenty of stew in it," he says.

A british tommy[120] was telling John Henry of the wonderfull{*sic*} acheivements{*sic*} of the British Forces. He listened for awhile but finally he could stand his boasts no longer so he said. "Well, you got nothing on the Yanks, We've got a gun that can shoot 105 miles and is so large that our general rides through the barrel of the gun in a Ford auto to inspect it." We were fed by the British when we were attached to them. Williams who is a big thin fellow said "I am going to volunteer to act as a scout, I am getting so thin I can hide behind a blade of grass and if a German sniper shoots at me, I'll just turn sideways and he won't be able to see me no how."

I was having great difficulty in making a French Y.M.C.A. worker under stand that I wanted some cigarettes. Lt Bates came along and said " I'll help you out I can speak French fluently." After making several gestures & mumbling a few words the madameselle{*sic*} said "Ah, Oui." She hurried away and returned shortly with two glasses of vin rouge.

After spending a restless night in a dugout I remarked "Gee there was something crawling over me about 8 inches long & 3 in high. It must have been a rat." "That wasn't a rat" said Harry Schell "That was a cootie, the rats here are 16 in long & 6 in high"

One of the recruits is terribly tounge{*sic*}-tied. He was writing a letter when Cpl. Robinson stopped near him to ask a question. He drawled & stuttered in an excited manner. His lips moved but he said nothing. Before he could answer the corporal walked away disgusted and remarked "If he writes the way he talks, the leuitenant{*sic*} will have an awful time, when he censors that letter.

It was my turn to take the sick, lame & lazy to the infirmary at sick call. I listened to the ailments of the men as they were called up individually by the army doctor. "What's the matter with you, sonny" he asked the first one on the list. "I have a pain in the stomach," he said. "Give him some pills" the doctor orders his assistant. "Take a black one & a white one every four hours." "Whats the matter with you, sonny He asks the next man. "I have an awful tooth ache" he answers sorrowfully. "Give him some pills & mark him Duty." He tells his assistant. Take a black one & a white one every four hours." He asks them all the same question and gives them all the same subscription{*sic*}, whether they have sore eyes, or a sprained ankle or a broken finger. They all get that "black one & a white one every four hours" It must take a man of great interlects{*sic*} and one who has devoted years of his life to the study of medicine & hygiene before he can become an army doctor.

One of the Batt runners came dashing into Hdqtrs breathing & excited "What's the trouble Baucher" he was asked. "I just ran into 3 Germans" he said "Why didn't you capture them" "An what was the use, they were dead"

We received our first bath in three months and were relieved of our old clothes & cooties. As we passed from the bath tent we received new & clean clothing and a blanket.

We were asked what size we were and then had the first thing that came handy thrown at us. That evening as we were laughing at each others appearance in our new outfit, Eiskart remarked. "The only thing that fits me is the blanket."

While I was resting comfortably in bed at the Base Hospital. An invalid soldier was carried in and placed in the bed next to mine. He looked pale and after the attendants left him he went off into a feint. We called the nurse and after a hurried examination She remarked "Poor fellow. He's a victim of shell shock. I've seen them act that way before." After working over him a few minutes, he came around all right and soon felt better. The nurse asked, "You are shell shock, Aren't you, sonny? Tell us how it happened." He looked up suprisingly{*sic*} and said "This is the closest I have been to the front"

While I was at Clamercy[121], I had my photo taken with a friend of mine. I conversed freely with the photographer and received very satisfactory service. Upon leaving the place my friend said to me "I didn't know you could speak French" "I can't" I told him. "Well how in the hell did you make him understand what you were talking about" he asked, puzzled. "Oh!" I said. "We spoke German"

The Captain inspecting quarters paused before Jones' bunk. "Don't you know better than to leave your shoe rag hanging over your bunk" Sir, that's not my shoe rag. That's my dish towel.

The sergt asked "All those that wish to go home, step forward."—"Company Halt!"

A man from the 82nd Div. sprung this.—The colonel attended a concert given by the Reg. Band. They were in the

midst of the strains of a snappy march when the colonel interrupted. Stop! Stop. where you are. Lets have a little unifor-
mity about this band. I want to see all those sliding trom-
bones come out to-gether{*sic*}."

Big Boy called "Jack! Oh Jack" "What the hell do you
want" I shouted. He said "Can't I call my dog without you
answering"

Abe Horowitz stood inspection cleanly shaven but forgot
to rub the Dier Kiss from his face. When the Lt gave him the
once over he shouted "Rub that stuff off your face. Where
do you think you are? In a beauty chorus?" Abe did as he was
told and kept his distance from the "Louie". The next day
he passed this same officer and failed to salute. "Come here,
you" he yelled "Don't you believe in saluting officers?" "Yes
sir," said Abe. "But I thought you were mad at me from yesterday."

Upon my second trip to the hospital I was fortunate to
get the bed next to Ben Goldstein. "How are you this morning Benny" asked the doctor upon this morning visit. "I
couldn't feel better in Hoboken" Benny told him.

Monahan was having great difficulty in finding the target
while we were on the range this morning. He had fired nine
times and received nine misses. He aimed his last shot and
the target went down and came up marked with a 2 on the
upper corner. Monahan called the Lieutenant and said "Sir
somebody else is shooting at my target."

Caputo was telling us about the first Regimental review
he experienced. He said "The Major was looking towards
me when he hollered "B'talion Attention". I am still wondering how he knew I was Italion{*sic*}."

"We will have 1/2 hour of setting up" announced Lt. Weaver. "I don't think I need it" protested Pat Emmert. "I set up two hours last night in a card game."

Dave Green in telling of his experiences in the army said "When I first got in the army we had bacon for breakfast pork for dinner ham for supper. To tell the truth, I never ate so much bread in my life before."

Davis & Wolf are always scrapping. They were at it while a group of men gathered around and watched. It was not long before Wolf complained that Davis was hitting below the belt. "Well, I can't help it" explained Davis. "He wears those English pants that come up to his arm pits."

We like to tell this one in the presence of an officer. Tom was walking down the street with his mind set on home. He noticed a child playing in the mud, moulding{sic} figures. An object that looked like a boat attracted Tom's attention, perhaps because he was interested in boats & transports. He also noticed figures of soldiers, some wearing corpls', others sergts' stripes. It would be a complete platoon if it had a Lt. So he asked the child why it did not make a Lieut. The child looked up and answered "Sir, the mud isn't thick enough to make a Lieut."

"Look at Ben Weber sitting down over there. Why his feet don't even touch the floor" I said. Oscar Meyerson remarked "A straight line is the shortest distance between two points. If his legs were straight instead of bowed, they would touch the floor"

While I was shaving this A.M. One of the fellows of the company, with whom I am not familiar approached me and asked "Are you from N.Y.C, Sarge" Alter I replied in the affirmative he said "There's one place I would like to see there and that is Mad. Sq. Garden". *"Why are* you so interested in that place? There are nicer places than Mad Sq. Garden in N.Y.C." I said "Well" he said. "I'd like to see some of those beautiful flowers they have there"

APPENDIX VII

GAS AS A CHEMICAL WEAPON IN WW I

The use of poisonous gas was first proposed in 1855 by Admiral Lord Dundonald to break the seige of Sevastopol. It was considered too barbaric to be employed. It was very difficult to target the victims effectively because of shifting winds. The initiators often became the victims. WW I marked the beginning of chemical warfare and the introduction of gas masks. The Germans were the first to use poisonous gas in April of 1915. The allies retaliated in September of 1915. Gas was the most feared weapon of WW I accounting for 25% of all American casualties.

These gases are roughly grouped according to the part of the body targeted. The three main categories of poisonous gases were lacrimators (tear gas), lung irritants (inducing pulmonary edema) and vesicants (blister gases). Although the use of gas in warfare has since been prohibited by international convention, modern military powers are still actively developing new ones. A modern example is the deadly nerve gas Sarin.

T-Stoff (xylyl bromide):
Was a non-lethal lachrymatory or tear gas. Its primary use was to cause a soldier to take off his gas mask to rub his eyes and thus end up inhaling a more toxic gas or to momentarily incapacitate the soldier at a critical moment making him an easier target for conventional weapons.

Chlorine Gas:
This is an example of a lung irritant. It is grayish-green in color with a distinctive odor. It was one of the more widely

used gases of WW I. Inhalation resulted in massive pulmonary edema with the victim essentially drowning in his own secretions.

Mustard Gas 1,1–thiobis(2-chloroethane)
Also known as H, pyprite and sulfur mustard. Mustard Gas became the name most widely used due to its having an odor similar to that of mustard, garlic or horseradish. This gas, along with Phosgene was the most dreaded gas used in WWI. Mustard Gas is a particularly deadly and debilitating poison. It essentially acts like vaporized acid causing reddening and blistering of the skin, blistering of the pulmonary lining when inhaled and destruction of the corneas of the eye resulting in blindness. Another reason this gas was so dreaded was that it could penetrate all protective materials and masks that they had available at the time. Any area of the body which was moist was particularly susceptible to attack because it is only slightly soluble in water making it difficult to wash off. As conditions in the trenches were soaking wet most of the time, this posed a serious problem.

Phosgene (Carbonyl Chloride):
Similar to Mustard Gas but not as commonly used. Brief exposure to as little as 50 parts per million can be fatal within an hour. It was too deadly and unpredictable to handle safely. Exposure to only 20 parts per million for as little as 1 minute resulted in severe irritation of the upper and lower respiratory tract along with burning throat, nausea, vomiting, chest pain, coughing, shortness of breath and headache. Pulmonary edema leading to cardiac failure usually followed within 4 to 72 hours after exposure.

END NOTES

[1] His brother Leo gave this first volume to Jack. This is written on the first page of the diary.

[2] Yaphank, Long Island, New York. Former site of Camp Upton (see below) . Present site of Brookhaven National Laboratories.

[3] Camp Upton located near Yaphank, Long Island. This was a major National Army training center for inductees from the New York City and Long Island area. Became the site of Brookhaven National Laboratory in 1947.

[4] Rosh Hashanah. Mr. Horn was Jewish.

[5] A "casual" is the term used for an enlisted man who has not yet undergone training

[6] Governor's Island is located in southeastern New York State in Upper New York Bay at the entrance to the East River, off the southern tip of Manhattan. It has an area of about 175 acres. Since 1755 the island has been reserved for military use, the oldest such establishment in the United States. Fort Jay was built there in 1794.

[7] Semaphora Drill. Early societies developed systems for sending simple messages or signals that could be seen or heard over a short distance, such as drumbeats, fire and smoke signals, or lantern beacons. Messages were attached to the legs of carrier pigeons that were released to fly home. This was the system used up until 1914 when World War I started.

Semaphore systems (visual codes) of flags or flashing lights were employed to send messages over relatively short but difficult to cross distances, such as from hilltop to hilltop, or between ships at sea. In the early 1790's the French scientist and engineer, Claude Chappe persuaded the French government to install a system of towers that used semaphore signals to send visual Telegraphs along approved routes throughout the country. The system was copied in Great Britain and the United States.

[8] The U.S. government financed WW I with debt not taxes. The debt was owed to those citizens, corporations etc. that purchased bonds. An interesting aside to this; the U.S. army sent more than 400,000 German helmets back to the U.S.A. which were given away to bond purchasers as an incentive. As a result there are probably more WW I German helmets in the U.S. than in Germany!

[9] Camp Gordon was in desperate need of recruits to train. This camp would receive the most difficult men from other camps such as Upton. These were often men who had trouble understanding English. Named for John Brown Gordon 1832-1904. He served as a General, as a Senator from Georgia and also Georgia's governor.

[10] The 59th Street Bridge (a.k.a. The Queensboro Bridge) connects midtown Manhattan with Queens

[11] The Manhattan Bridge connects western Brooklyn with southeastern Manhattan.

[12] The Williamsburgh Bridge (a.k.a. The Delancy Street Bridge) connects Brooklyn with the Lower East Side of Manhattan.

[13] The Brooklyn Bridge spans the East River and connects Manhattan Island to the western shore of Brooklyn.

[14] John Pilkington and Henry Threlfall Wilson first founded the White Star Line in Liverpool in 1845. World War I hurt White Star as it did other shipping lines. Not much income could be generated during the war years with most of White Star's ships either tied up in military service or getting picked off by German submarines and mine fields. There was an immense shortage of firemen and coal stokers during the war as well as a shortage of coal itself. Most had been recruited into military service. In 1927, the White Star Line was returned to British interests, and normal operations were intended to begin. White Star owned the Titanic.

[15] The *Justica* was newly commissioned in 1917 and was sunk by a German torpedo the next year.

[16] From the French bouillie (boiled). Boiled beef sealed in cans was a staple ration during the Great War.

[17] Fritz. One of the many slang expressions used during that time for Germans. Boche and Gerry were common in WW I. The derogatory term "Kraut" does not appear to have come into use until WW II.

[18]Audriq

[19] The Lewis gun was a British light machine gun that was gas operated, air cooled, and fed by a horizontal rotating drum containing 47 or 97 rounds. This weapon was an improved design by I.N. Lewis of the U.S. Army of an already existing gun. In 1914, at the outbreak of WW I, the Birmingham Small Arms Company of Birmingham, England began manufacturing the weapon. The gun could be used as both a

ground weapon and an aircraft gun. The Lewis gun became standard issue to the Allied Forces in France. Each platoon had it's own Lewis Gunners. It is believed that Cedric Popkin using a Lewis Gun finally shot down the Red Baron.

[20] Audriq

[21] La Marseillaise. The French national anthem.

[22] Mondicourt Station

[23] Location of Army Evacuation Hospital

[24] Location of the 77th Division Headquarters

[25] Decoration Day was the original name for what is now Memorial Day. Decoration Day began after the Civil War when women in the North and South, in a gesture of impartiality, decorated the graves of both Confederate and Union soldiers with flowers. This practice caught on around the country and people began to place flowers on the graves of all dead soldiers from American wars. In 1868, General John A. Lugan, commander-in-chief of the Grand Army of the Republic, declared May 30 be set aside as a special day each year to honor America's war dead. In 1968, the observance of Memorial Day was changed to May 31.

[26]Spinal Meningitis. This is an inflammation or infection of the membranes surrounding the brain and\or spinal cord. In wartime this condition generally results from a head wound or perforating spinal injury thus allowing bacteria into the spinal fluid. In the early part of the 20th century this most certainly would have been fatal.

[27] Sergeant Horn registered for the draft on June 5, 1917 and was drafted on June 20, 1917.

[28] Gezaincourt

[29] Bernaville

[30] Ailly-Le-Haut-Clocher

[31] Usually spelled aerodromes. British word first used in 1908. Aerodromes are what would be the early equivalents of airports, airfields, airbases etc.

[32] Saint Remy

[33] Amiens; Location on August 8, 1918 where the German front line was overwhelmed by an Armada of British and French tanks. The so-called "Black Day of the German Army".

[34] Unsure of this one. Cannot be found on any maps of France.

[35] Probably Oise.

[36] Thaon

[37] Giercourt

[38] Rambervillers

[39] Mesnil. This was the only place that the Germans had a foothold across the Meuse River. They first took it in late September 1914. It was retaken four years later by the U.S. in September 1918.

[40] Baccarat. One week was spent there by the regiment in training.

[41] St. Maurice. The new Battalion Headquarters after Pas.

[42] N.A. National Army

[43] Boche. Derogatory slang term for Germans.

[44] Neuviller

[45] Indian Village. Cannot find on any map.

[46] Moyen. Possible misspelling as this cannot be found

[47] Chauchat rifle. French rifle first produced in 1915. This rifle is considered the predecessor of the modern assault rifle. It was the first to have a pistol grip in the front with an inline shoulder stock in the rear, a large capacity magazine, single-fire or automatic selector switch and a bipod. This was the most manufactured automatic weapon of World War I, out-numbering every other machine gun made by the Allies and the Central Powers. The French and AEF Chauchat gunner teams formed the nucleus of the world's first infantry machine gun teams.

[48] Elsie Janis born Elsie Bierbowere March 16, 1889, Columbus, Ohio died February 26, 1956, Los Angeles, California. She was a rather popular writer, actress, composer and production manager

[49] Military abbreviation for Olive Drab

[50] Slang expression for German. Usually spelled Gerry.

[51] Strombos Horn. A huge air horn used for alarming the troops to danger such as a gas attack etc.

[52] Serainville

[53] Neufchateau

[54] La Ferte Gaucher

[55]Fère-en-Tardenois

[56] A pyrotechnic signal in a system of signaling using white or colored balls of fire projected from a special firing device. Invented by Edward W. Very, an American Naval Officer who died in 1910.

[57] Possibly Bruay-en-Artois

[58] Post of Command. Sometimes the same place as the headquarters of an organization. Generally in combat the headquarters and supplies are left behind in some convenient place where it can function without annoyance from the enemy, while the Commanding Officer, with part of his staff go forward to be nearer the front line that he may better direct the operations. This forward location or headquarters is called the "Post of Command" or P.C.

[59] Fismes

[60] Stir-it coffee. Apparently an early ancestor to modern day instant coffee.

[61] Glennes

[62] Camp Le Chatelier

[63] A word of explanation pointing to the difference between the meanings of the terms The Argonne and the Argonne forest. The former refers to the whole region between the Aisne and the Meuse rivers, largely open country, though with small patches of woods; while the latter refers to a very dense and continuous woodland some twelve kilometers at its widest point from east to west and thirty kilometers from north to south.

[64] Florent

[65] Aire River. A stream some fifty feet across and eight to ten feet deep was strongly held by the Germans and was a barrier to the 77th Division's progress.

[66] The Mudros Armistice occurred on October 30, 1918, at the port of Mudros on the Aegean island of Lemnos. The treaty was signed between the Allied forces, represented by Great Britain and the Ottoman Empire. This marked their defeat in WW I as well as the end of the Ottoman Empire. The armistice also guaranteed Allied control of the strategic Transcaucasian areas and also Allied access to the Black Sea.

[67] The Witching Waves was a ride invented by Theophilus Van Kennel. It was installed at Coney Island in 1907. It consisted of a large oval course with a flexible metal floor. By using a system of reciprocating levers beneath the floor, the ride generated a continuous wavelike motion followed by another in the flexible floor without the actual floor moving forward. The undulating floor propelled steerable small cars seating two passengers forward. It was fascinating to watch and a popular fun ride.

[68] The Austrians opened Armistice negotiations in the field on November 1st and instituted a cease-fire on Novem-

ber 3rd. The Italians did not recognize the cease-fire until the next day. During this interval, 300,000 Austrian troops were captured.

[69] The Kaiser was William II born in Berlin (1859-1941). He became Emperor of Germany after the death of his father Frederick III in 1888. He was also the King of Prussia (1888-1918). It was his policies that helped to bring about WW I. He was a proponent of the Triple Alliance of Germany, Austria-Hungary and Italy. He felt that this alliance would serve as a deterrent to war, but ironically it was his confused and contradictory policies that aggravated the international frictions which led to WW I. After the German offensive of 1918 failed, the German armies and people began to turn against him. William was forced to abdicate his throne and spend the rest of his life secluded in the Netherlands.

[70] Although celebrated yearly on this date, Armistice Day was not made a legal holiday until 1938 when Congress officially voted it. After the Second World War, Armistice Day continued to be observed on November 11. In 1953, the little town of Emporia, Kansas called the holiday "Veterans' Day". In recognition of the veterans of both wars soon a bill was introduced and passed by Congress to rename the holiday Veterans' Day. Veterans of Korea and Vietnam are now included in the remembrances of Veterans' Day. It was hoped that this holiday would remind us of the sacrifices that were made so that we could enjoy freedom.

[71] Chalons-sur-Marne

[72] Most likely *Table d'Hôte* meaning Guest Table. A French tradition which has fallen out of use, whereby a table was set

aside for those who would otherwise be dining alone or for out-of-town visitors to sit together.

[73] American Expeditionary Force

[74] Café de la Guerre

[75] Dijon

[76] Probably the same as "Bully Beef ".

[77] Froggies. A somewhat derogatory name for French people in general. Thought to be based upon the French propensity for eating frog meat.

[78] Chaumont

[79] Buisson

[80] La Ferte-sur-Aube

[81] Partir tout de suite. French for "To leave right away".

[82] Dinteville

[83] Aix-les-Bains

[84] Clamecy

[85] Chalon-sur-Saône

[86] Invented by Sir Wilfris Stokes in 1915. It consisted of a smoothbore barrel with a closed end, resting on a baseplate and held up at an angle of 45 degrees by a bipod. A screw mechanism allowed the barrel to be adjusted for angles of

elevation. It fired a simple cylindrical bomb with a perforated tube at the rear end into which a shotgun cartridge filled with gunpowder was fitted. The bomb was dropped down the barrel to strike a firing pin fixed at the base; this ignited the shotgun cartridge and the explosion of the powder ejected the bomb. The first bombs used weighed about 4.5 pounds and had a range of about 900 meters. Later bombs were lighter with a correspondingly longer range. The Stokes mortars were an indirect fire support weapon firing up and over friendly trenches to land in the enemy's trenches. In addition to explosive rounds, they also fired smoke rounds, which hid the user's position from enemy observation and fire allowing coverage of troop movement and attack. They were also used to distract the enemy into thinking that an attack was coming from the wrong direction thus drawing enemy troops away from the real attacks.

[87] French infinitive for "to leave".

[88] La Roche-sur-Yon.

[89] This hotel still exists and is now called the Rochester Champs Élysées, 92 Rue La Boetie.

[90] He is probably referring to the Champs Élysées especially in light of the location of the hotel.

[91] Avant la guerre; Before the war

[92] Boulevard de la Madeleine, Île-de-France, Paris

[93] French adverb for "How much".

[94] Coucher. French infinitive for "to go to bed"
[95] Sablé

[96] Poillé

[97] Fontenay

[98] Angers

[99] American Red Cross

[100] Le Pont Transbordeur. Tram bridge across the Loire River opened October 28, 1903. Designed by Ferdinand Arnodin (1845-1924). Spans a distance of 142 meters and carries 250-300 people with each transit at a speed of 5 kilometers\hour which takes about 2 minutes.

[101]Profane military expression meaning "Shit Out of Luck".

[102] Knights of Columbus

[103] Le Hotel Pavillion, 54 Rue Saint Dominique, Paris

[104] Probably the Soldier's and Sailor's Club.

[105] Le Pantheon. Built as a church by Louis XV. Took 31 years to build and was completed in 1789. Converted to a mausoleum for great Frenchmen.

[106] Le Hotel Notre Dame, 51 Rue de Malte, Paris

[107] Perhaps furlough

[108] Montparnasse/Bienvenüe

[109] Avoise

[110] Major General Robert A. Alexander. Led the 77th Division from August 31, 1918 until November 11, 1918 (Armistice Day)

[111] Main embarkation center along with Sablé.

[112] Regimental

[113] American Expeditionary Commander

[114] Fontenay

[115] Must mean the piers on the waterfront docks at Brest.

[116] Most likely they saw Sandy Hook Lighthouse located on a small peninsula jutting into Raritan Bay off the New Jersey coast.

[117] Camp Mills was located in Mineola, Long Island, New York. It served originally as the training camp for the 42nd division. In early 1918 it was put into service as a port. It could handle up to 40,000 men. This camp served as a source of experienced officers for Camp Upton.

[118] A.W.O.C.. may represent a joke based on A.W.O.L.(absent without leave) meaning absent without caring.

[119] Quarter Master

[120] Somewhat redundant. 'Tommy " was a slang term of affection for a British foot soldier.

[121] Clamecy